Over the Moon

COMPLETE PRIMARY ENGLISH LANGUAGE PROGRAMME

GW01220198

OUT OF THIS WORLD

5th CLASS Reader

MAUREEN HOEY

GILL EDUCATION

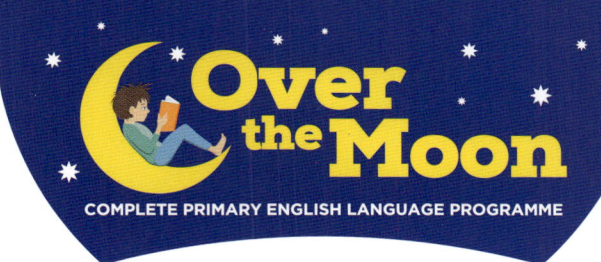

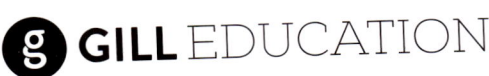

Gill Education
Hume Avenue
Park West
Dublin 12
www.gilleducation.ie

Gill Education is an imprint of M.H. Gill & Co.

© Maureen Hoey 2020

ISBN: 978-0-7171-85917

All rights reserved. No part of this publication may be copied, reproduced or transmitted in any form or by any means without written permission of the publishers or else under the terms of any licence permitting limited copying issued by the Irish Copyright Licensing Agency.

Editor: Kristin Jensen
Proofreader: Denise Dwyer
Original series design: Liz White Designs
Design and layout: Síofra Murphy
Illustrations: Mike Garton, Katie Kear, Sonya Abby Soekarno, Tika and Tata/The Bright Agency

For permission to reproduce photographs, the authors and publisher gratefully acknowledge the following:

© Alamy: 6, 7, 9, 10, 63, 114, 116, 119, 143; © Getty Images: 11, 12; © iStock: 3, 4, 5, 13, 14, 15, 16, 29, 80, 84, 88, 96, 121, 122, 123, 124, 125, 126, 129, 130, 131, 132, 133, 134, 138; © Shutterstock: 10; © Wikimedia Commons: 7.

The paper used in this book is made from the wood pulp of managed forests. For every tree felled, at least one tree is planted, thereby renewing natural resources.

The authors and publisher are grateful to the following for permission to reproduce copyrighted material:

Excerpt from *Genius! The Most Astonishing Inventions of All Time* by Deborah Kespert. Copyright © 2015 Thames & Hudson Ltd., London. Reprinted by kind permission of Thames & Hudson Ltd. 'Sparks' by Mark C. Bird. Copyright © Mark C. Bird, ps4k.com. Reprinted by permission of the author. 'World's Largest Beach Clean-Up: Trash Ridden to Pristine In Two Years' by Joe McCarthy, EcoWatch, 2017. Copyright © Joe McCarthy. 'Mrs World: A Global Warning' and 'Different' from *Vanishing Trick*, originally published by Frances Lincoln Children's Books in 2015. Copyright © Ros Asquith 2015. Selected text excerpts and art from pages 2–14 from *Regarding the Fountain* by Kate Klise. Illustrated by Sarah M. Klise. Text copyright 1998 by Kate Klise, illustration copyright 1998 Sarah M. Klise. 'The Drinking Fountain' from *When the Teacher's Isn't Looking* by Kenn Nesbitt, copyright © 2010. Reprinted by permission of Running Press Kids, an imprint of Hachette Book Group, Inc. Excerpt and illustrations from *Dying to Meet You: 43 Old Cemetery Road* by Kate Klise, illustrated by Sarah M. Klise. Text copyright © 2009 by Kate Klise. Illustrations copyright © 2009 by Sarah M. Klise. Reprinted by permission of Houghton Mifflin Harcourt Publishing Company. All rights reserved. 'The Ghost Teacher' by Allan Ahlberg from *Puffin Book of Utterly Brilliant Poetry*, 1999. Copyright © Allan Ahlberg. Extract from *Out of My Mind* by Sharon M. Draper. Copyright © 2010 Sharon M. Draper. Reprinted with the permission of Atheneum Books for Young Readers, an imprint of Simon and Schuster Children's Publishing Division. All rights reserved. *The Lion, the Witch and the Wardrobe* by C.S. Lewis, copyright © C.S. Lewis Pte. Ltd. 1950. Illustrations by Pauline Baynes © copyright C.S. Lewis Pte Ltd. 1950. Reprinted by permission. 'The Door' by Miroslav Holub. Copyright © Miroslav Holub. *Poems Before & After: Collected English Translations*, trans. Ian & Jarmila Milner et al. (Bloodaxe Books, 2006). Excerpt and book cover image from *Where the Mountain Meets the Moon* by Grace Lin, copyright © 2009. Reprinted by permission of Little, Brown and Company, an imprint of Hachette Book Group, Inc. 'Dragon Dance' by Max Fatchen. Copyright © The Estate of Max Fatchen 1989. Reproduced with the kind permission of Johnson & Alcock Ltd. 'Dave Dirt's Christmas Presents' by Kit Wright. Copyright © Kit Wright. 'Computer Boot' by Kenn Nesbitt. Copyright © Kenn Nesbitt, 2009. All rights reserved. *You Wouldn't Want to Be in the Trenches in World War One!* © The Salariya Book Company Ltd, 2014. Reprinted with permission. 'Space Explained' © Primary Planet Children's News Magazine. 'Asteroid' poems by Elaine Magliaro. Copyright © Elaine Magliaro, *Things to Do*, 2017. Reprinted by permission of the author. *Volcano Rising* text copyright © 2013 by Elizabeth Rusch. Illustrations copyright © 2013 by Susan Swan. Used with permission by Charlesbridge Publishing, Inc. 85 Main Street, Watertown, MA 02472. All rights reserved. 'How to Care for a Dog' text reproduced with permission of the RSPCA. 'Greedy Dog' by James Hurley from *100 Best Poems for Children* edited by Roger McGough. Copyright © James Hurley, published by Puffin, 2002. 'Trickery' extract from *101 Things to Do Before You Grow Up* by Laura Dower. Copyright © Weldon Owen International. 'Tricks' from *Spots in My Eyes* by Michael Rosen (© Michael Rosen, 1983). Printed by permission of United Agents (www.unitedagents.co.uk) on behalf of Michael Rosen. 'Interview with Chris Van Allsburg' transcribed from the video 'Chris Van Allsburg on Drawing and Writing', copyright © Educurious. 'How to Play the Jumanji Board Game' adapted from top5reviewed.com and twinfinite.net. 'Jumanji' by Eleanor Kellett, hellopoetry.com. Copyright © Eleanor Kellett. Text excerpt and book cover image from *World's Strangest Predators*, 1st edn. Permission from Lonely Planet © 2018, Lonely Planet. Extract from *13 Buildings Children Should Know* by Annette Roeder, 2009, published by Prestel. Copyright © Annette Roeder. 'Oh, How I'd Like to Travel' by Jodi Right, poemhunter.com. Copyright © Jodi Right. Extract from *Young Heroes* by Lula Bridgeport. Reproduced by permission of Stripes Publishing Limited. Text Copyright © Lula Bridgeport, 2018. Illustrations copyright © Frederica Frenna, Isabel Munoz and Julianna Swaney, 2018. 'Wendy Wise' by Kenn Nesbitt from *My Cat Knows Karate*. Copyright © Kenn Nesbitt, 2018. All rights reserved.

The authors and publisher have made every effort to trace all copyright holders, but if any have been inadvertently overlooked we would be pleased to make the necessary arrangement at the first opportunity.

Contents

Unit	Text	Genre and Theme	Reading Goal	Poem	Page
1 Non-fiction	*Genius! The Most Astonishing Inventions of All Time* by Deborah Kespert	Recount (Inventions)	Determine the important points as I read.	'Sparks' by Mark C. Bird	1
2 Non-fiction	*Eco News* by Joe McCarthy	Recount (The Environment)	Read on, use textual and pictorial evidence to determine and clarify the meaning of the phrases.	'Mrs World: A Global Warning' by Ros Asquith	9
3 Fiction	*Regarding the Fountain* by Kate Klise	Writing to Socialise (Water)	Use my tone of voice to match the character's mood.	'The Drinking Fountain' by Kenn Nesbitt	17
4 Fiction	*Dying to Meet You* by Kate Klise	Writing to Socialise (Hallowe'en)	Vary my tone and use pitch to express the mood of the characters.	'The Ghost Teacher' by Allan Ahlberg	25
5 Fiction	*Out of My Mind* by Sharon Draper	Narrative (At School)	Pay attention to commas – pause for a breath, then read on.	'Different' by Ros Asquith	33
6 Fiction	*The Lion, the Witch and the Wardrobe* by C.S. Lewis	Narrative (Adventure)	Examine how speech marks are used and how question marks affect the tone of voice.	'The Door' by Miroslav Holub	41
7 Fiction	*Where the Mountain Meets the Moon* by Grace Lin	Narrative (Legends)	Read for deeper meaning.	'Dragon Dance' by Max Fatchen	49
8 Fiction	*A Christmas Carol* by Charles Dickens	Narrative (Christmas)	Develop fluency through repeated practice.	'Dave Dirt's Christmas Presents' by Kit Wright	57
9 Non-fiction	*Gaming*	Persuasive Writing (Gaming)	Pay close attention to the tone of the author (for example, is it serious, dismissive, formal, optimistic?), as the tone can be used to influence or persuade the reader.	'Computer Boot' by Ken Nesbitt	65

Unit	Title	Genre	Reading Goal	Poem	Page
10 Non-fiction	*You Wouldn't Want to Be in the Trenches in World War One!* by Alex Woolf	Persuasive Writing (World War One)	Visualise to understand and learn what it was like to be in the trenches.	'In Flanders Fields' by John McCrae	73
11 Non-fiction	*Space Explained* by Primary Planet Magazine	Explanation (Space)	Read for information.	'Asteroids' by Elaine Magliaro and Cinquain Poem	81
12 Non-fiction	*Volcano Rising* by Elizabeth Rusch	Explanation (Volcanoes)	Monitor my understanding by paying attention to my reading and use the diagrams/pictures to aid me.	'Volcano' from sciencepoems.net	89
13 Non-fiction	*How to Care for a Dog* by the RSPCA	Procedure (Pets)	Notice how procedural texts use verbs to give readers a clear understanding of how to do something.	'Greedy Dog' by James Hurley	97
14 Non-fiction	*Trickery* from *101 Things to Do Before You Grow Up* by Laura Dower	Procedure (Magic Tricks)	Pay attention to the sequence of instructions in order to do the tricks.	'Tricks' by Michael Rosen	105
15 Non-fiction	*Jumanji*	Procedure (Board Games)	Notice the structure and word choice in board game instructions to help me understand the game.	'Jumanji' by Eleanor Kellett	113
16 Non-fiction	*World's Strangest Predators*	Report (Predators)	Determine important information.	'Predator' from sciencepoems.net	121
17 Non-fiction	*13 Buildings Children Should Know* by Annette Roeder	Report (Famous Buildings)	Re-read information to self-correct.	'Oh, How I'd Like to Travel' by Jodi Right	129
18 Non-fiction	*Young Heroes* by Lula Bridgeport	Report (Famous People)	Understand and determine what makes a sporting hero.	'Wendy Wise' by Kenn Nesbitt	137

Recount

Ella's Intro

Dia daoibh, a chairde. Tá failte romhaibh chuig Over the Moon *Rang A Cúig! Tá súil agam gur bhain gach duine taitneamh as an samhradh.* (Hello, friends. Welcome to *Over the Moon* Fifth Class. I hope everyone enjoyed the summer.)

I have such an exciting unit for you to read. We are going to begin by looking at **recount** writing. A recount is the retelling of an event or an experience. Examples can be found in diaries, newspaper articles, emails and history books.

We are going to look at a recount by examining three geniuses who created some of the most astonishing inventions of all time. My *Over the Moon* friends have come along to introduce their favourite inventions.

The inventor of the modern ejector seat was an Irishman.

The Montgolfier brothers were the geniuses who invented the hot air balloon. I can't wait to take a ride in one someday!

Nancy Johnson invented the ice cream maker. What a super invention!

I love taking pictures. John Joly was the genius behind colour photography.

Let's read on to find out about the geniuses who created the earthquake detector, flying machines and the World Wide Web!

Transfer of skills: An invention is a unique or novel device, method or process. Many inventions have changed our lives. Do you know what the word 'invention' is in another language? Do you notice any similarities?

aireagán (Irish), *wynalazek* (Polish), *invención* (Spanish), *l'invention* (French)

> My reading goal ★ Determine the important points as I read.

Genius! The Most Astonishing Inventions of All Time

Detecting Earthquakes

THE BIG IDEA	To invent a clever mechanical device that could tell if there was an earthquake and which direction it was coming from.
CHALLENGES No one knew what caused earthquakes. Enemies claimed that the device did not work.	**WHAT:** Earthquake detector **WHO:** Zhang Heng **WHERE:** China **WHEN:** Around 132 **HOW:** He was skilled at working with moving parts and gears. **WHY:** He was fascinated by the Earth, planets, moon and stars.
BACKGROUND	Zhang Heng lived during the Han Dynasty (206 BCE to 220 CE). At this time, China was far ahead of Europe in developing machines. He worked for two emperors as chief **astronomer** and was also a poet.

NAME: Zhang Heng
BORN: Around 78
DIED: Aged about 61
NATIONALITY: Chinese
JOB: Astronomer, mathematician
FAMOUS FOR: Being one of China's most brilliant scientists, with many inventions to his name

INVENTIONS
Made a planetary sphere, or globe, that showed the planets moving.
Built an earthquake detector, or seismoscope, that made a sound when the Earth shook.

ACHIEVEMENT
Named and catalogued stars. Worked out that the moon does not make its own light.

What New Mechanical Marvel Would Zhang Heng Show to the Emperor?

When Zhang Heng presented his beautiful metal earthquake detector to the emperor, he already had a long track record as an incredible inventor. He had designed a globe to show the movement of planets and the stars, improved the design of the water clock and built a mechanical trundle cart that could also measure the distance a vehicle travelled. He had also developed all kinds of complicated mathematical calculations, planned calendars and written poetry. In short, Zhang Heng was an all-round genius.

His latest revolutionary device was shaped like a vase with dragon heads at the top and frogs at the bottom. Inside, a **pendulum**, or swinging weight, moved when the Earth shook and sent a ball from one of the dragons into a frog's mouth. Depending on which frog the ball fell into, you could tell which direction the earthquake was coming from.

In ancient China, people feared earthquakes hugely and believed that they were punishments from the heavens. Today, we know that an earthquake is a shaking of the Earth's crust caused by movements in the giant plates on which our **continents** and oceans sit.

The first time Zhang Heng demonstrated his machine, it sprang into action. But no one felt the ground tremble, so his enemies said that it didn't work. Then several days later, a messenger arrived announcing that there had indeed been an earthquake about 500 km away in the direction indicated by the machine.

Zhang Heng's machine could not predict when an earthquake was going to happen, and even today predicting earthquakes is difficult. But we do have modern equipment called **seismometers** that record vibrations in the Earth. When the vibrations increase, it means an earthquake is more likely.

Although Zhang Heng's device was simple by modern standards, it was incredible for its time. What's more, no one else managed to make an effective earthquake detector until the eighteenth century – more than 1,500 years later.

> DANGER! Many earthquakes have hit China, including the world's deadliest earthquake. It took place in 1556 and killed over 800,000 people.

Many modern buildings, like these tall office blocks and skyscrapers in Taiwan, are designed to stay up when an earthquake occurs.

Flying Machines

THE BIG IDEA	To design astonishing machines that would allow human beings to take to the air and fly.
CHALLENGES Getting a flying machine off the ground before the engine had been invented.	**WHAT:** Ornithopter and helicopter **WHO:** Leonardo da Vinci **WHERE:** Vinci, present-day Italy **WHEN:** 1480s **HOW:** He studied how birds flew and sketched their wings. **WHY:** He was obsessed with the idea of flight from an early age.
BACKGROUND	Da Vinci trained as a painter and soon became famous because he was so talented. Throughout his life, he <u>furiously filled</u> notebooks with designs for different inventions.

NAME: Leonardo da Vinci
BORN: 15 April 1452
DIED: Aged 67
NATIONALITY: Florentine
JOB: Artist, sculptor, architect
FAMOUS FOR: Painting the *Mona Lisa*

INVENTIONS
Drew designs for flying machines, including one with flapping wings called an ornithopter.
Sketched other inventions, including a submarine and an armoured tank.

ACHIEVEMENT
Recognised as one of the greatest artists of all time.

Would Da Vinci Achieve His Dream and Build a Machine That Could Fly?

Leonardo da Vinci

During the fifteenth century, while Leonard da Vinci painted fabulous works of art and was admired for his <u>wide-ranging talents</u>, he was also trying to fulfil a dream. He wanted to build a flying machine. Stories tell us that a bird landed on his cradle as a baby and its tail feathers brushed his face. Could this have inspired his **obsession** with flight?

<u>For decades</u>, da Vinci studied the movement of birds, drew sketches and experimented with different designs. In secret, he recorded these ideas in notebooks, making more than 500 drawings on the topic. He came up with designs for lots of other things too, including a giant crossbow, a submarine, a robot knight that could lift its helmet and an ideal city for the future. By the time he died, he had filled over 13,000 pages.

Da Vinci's notebooks were not published during his lifetime, neither were they bound like the books we know today. Instead, they were loose sheets of paper bundled together in cloth. They were difficult to read because he used a special back-to-front mirror writing to keep important ideas secret. When da Vinci died, pages fell into the hands of friends and collectors. In 1966, two notebooks turned up in a museum in Spain, more than 500 years after he had written them!

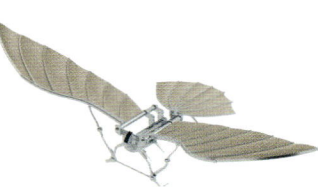

A model of Leonardo da Vinci's flying machine.

One of da Vinci's ideas for a flying machine was a bird-like **contraption** with mechanical flapping wings operated by a human being. Today, we call a machine like this an **ornithopter**. Da Vinci came up with several designs for ornithopters. One had a spinning wing on top and lifted straight off the ground. It was the first design for a helicopter. No one is really sure, but da Vinci's idea may have been inspired by the seeds of the sycamore tree, which whirl as they fall, or perhaps an Archimedes screw. The first working helicopters were not mass-produced until the 1940s, almost 500 years after da Vinci's sketch.

Leonardo da Vinci's flying machines were wildly imaginative, but there was a big problem. They were too heavy. Even with ropes, cranks and **pulleys**, a human being could never produce enough power to get them off the ground.

Imagine if Leonardo da Vinci was alive today and walked with his 'eyes turned skywards'. He might see skydivers making daredevil parachute jumps, helicopters reporting on traffic conditions or passenger planes flying to far-off places. He would discover that his sketches had flown in a space probe to Mars and were wandering around the surface of the planet in the Curiosity rover! How might he feel to know that after all this time, his dreams about flying had become real?

A modern-day helicopter usually has four narrow blades on top to provide lift. Tail blades stop the helicopter from spinning round in the air.

The Arrival of the Internet

THE BIG IDEA	A new way to communicate – to let people see and share information on any computer, anywhere in the world.
CHALLENGES Keeping the web a free, fair and safe space for everybody to use and enjoy.	**WHAT:** World Wide Web **WHO:** Tim Berners-Lee **WHERE:** England **WHEN:** 1991 **HOW:** By thinking big and connecting lots of ideas. **WHY:** He hopes it will help people to understand each other better.
BACKGROUND	The World Wide Web is part of the internet. In the 1960s, computer scientists in the United States created a small network of computers called ARPANET. It inspired the internet that we know today.

NAME: Tim Berners-Lee
BORN: 8 June 1955
NATIONALITY: English
JOB: Computer scientist
FAMOUS FOR: Inventing the World Wide Web

INVENTIONS
Designed a system that connected information and let people share web pages.
Came up with the name World Wide Web (www.), which is used for all website addresses today.

ACHIEVEMENT
Helped to make the internet a huge part of our daily lives.

How Did Tim Berners-Lee Achieve This?

In 1990, Tim Berners-Lee worked in a **laboratory** in Europe called CERN. Today, this is where the Large Hadron Collider smashes tiny **particles** together to find out about the universe. Scientists come from all over the world to research there. Back then, Berners-Lee discovered an annoying problem. Many of the computers had different **software**, so it was very difficult for the scientists to share their work.

Tim Berners-Lee

Frustrated by this, he came up with the idea for a system that would link the information together so that everyone at CERN could see it. Then, as he worked on his project, it dawned on him that he could do something much bigger. His system could reach the whole world, not just the people at CERN. It could be a World Wide Web. Initially, Berners-Lee had a different name for it – Information Mesh. But he was worried that it sounded too much like Information 'Mess'.

In December 1990, Tim Berners-Lee created the first web browser. In August 1991, he put it on the internet. Berners-Lee also provided a website that explained the browser and showed how to use it.

Many inventions are built and sold to make money, but the World Wide Web was free for everyone to develop. It grew at a lightning pace. Today, through the World Wide Web, we can learn things, play games, shop, stay in touch with friends and share our ideas. It has changed our daily lives and is one of the most powerful ways in the world for us to communicate with each other.

▶▶ **HOW ...**
A Web Browser Works

❶ When you type in the web address, your web browser finds the computer that hosts, or stores, the website. It could be anywhere in the world!

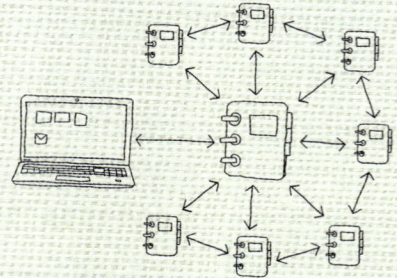

❷ Your browser asks your local computer server first. This is just like a big telephone directory full of contacts.

❸ These contacts ask more contacts until one finds the website and pings it back to you the way you found it. It all happens in a few seconds or less.

Ella's Response

Are you inspired? We have read about only three geniuses and some of the most astonishing inventions of all time, but there are many more you could read about and research.

Nikola Tesla

Karl and Bertha Benz

Stephanie Kwolek

Johannes Gutenberg

Grace Hopper

One of my favourite inventions is flavoured potato crisps. Joseph 'Spud' Murphy developed cheese and onion flavoured crisps in 1954. They taste so good, but I could live without them.

What is your favourite invention? What invention could you not live without?

I hope you enjoyed your first unit!

Author's Intent

Do you think the author, Deborah Kespert, wrote this to inform, persuade or entertain us?

What do you think of her structure? Did it make it easier for you to understand the text?

Sparks

by Mark C. Bird

From Pac-Man, Oz, the moonwalk, Jaws
To rockets and sliced bread
Once sparks that lit up question marks
Ideas in human heads ...

The PS3, Xbox and Wii
The BMX, the kite
King Kong, Ping Pong and hip hop songs
The book, to read and write

The Pyramids, New York, Madrid
The submarine, the chair
The bed, cheese spread and Barbie's head
The wheel, the bulb, the square

The swimming pool, the slide, the school
The fizzy pop, the gum
The shoe, kung fu, the flushing loo
The phone, the clock, the drum

The microchip, the paper clip
Cartoons, the ball, the screw
Blue jeans, baked beans and trampolines
The toothbrush, pens, shampoo

The aeroplane, ice-cream, champagne
The world wide web, the fridge
French fries, cat's eyes and custard pies
The road, the car, the bridge

Wonder what's in your head
Magnify the sparks
Imagine what you will invent
With your own question marks

Recount

The Environment

Evan's Intro

Evan @emk1

Hi, everyone! We are already on our second unit. I have my environmentalist hat on. Do you remember the extract on plastics from Third Class?

1:14 PM – 16 Sep   11 Likes

Tom @tck15
Replying to @Evan

I do! Remember my motto? 'Do something drastic, cut the plastic!'
You reposted
TCK@BDG

Remember this when you use plastic next time!
#Beachcleanup #Mumbai #India #Ocean

Evan @emk1
Replying to @Tom

That photo makes me so mad! All that plastic. My mum has stopped buying plastic milk cartons. Every little bit helps! Did you hear about Afroz Shah? He's formidable. We're going to read a news report about him. Can you remember the features of a news report?

Tom @tck15
Replying to @Evan

A headline, the reporter's name, an introduction, information about the main events in chronological order, photos with captions … Can't wait to read it!

Transfer of skills: Rubbish is becoming a big problem for us and for the environment. Do you know what the word 'rubbish' is in another language? Let's take a look.

bruscar (Irish), *lixo* (Portuguese), *basura* (Spanish), *ordures* (French)

My reading goal ★ Read on, use textual and pictorial evidence to determine and clarify the meaning of the phrases.

Eco News

World's Largest Beach Clean-Up: Trash Ridden to Pristine in Two Years

By Joe McCarthy

A lot of people take part in community clean-up efforts – spending a Saturday morning picking up litter in a park, mowing an overgrown field or painting a fence. But not everyone has the drive to do what a young lawyer and **environmentalist** in Mumbai recently accomplished.

In 2015, Afroz Shah moved to an apartment near Versova Beach, an ignored strip of ocean near **slums**. He was shocked by the pollution that he saw – the beach was covered in rotting garbage. Nobody could walk along the beach, let alone swim in the water, without being <u>assaulted by the smell</u>.

'The plastic was 5.5 feet high. A man could <u>drown in the plastic</u>,' Shah told CNN. 'I said I'm going to come on the field and do something. I have to protect my environment and it requires <u>ground action</u>.'

At first, Shah and his neighbour, an 84-year-old man, would go out and pick up as much trash as they could. After a while, Shah realised that he had to expand his team if he was going to make a dent in what was essentially an environmental crisis. He began knocking on doors and talking with local residents, explaining the harm caused by marine pollution. His determination inspired a lot of people and soon dozens, hundreds and eventually more than a thousand volunteers from all walks of life pitched in.

Clean-ups were ironically called 'dates with the ocean' because they were really arduous affairs, 'shin-deep in rotting garbage under the scorching Indian sun', according to the UN.

Heave ho! The United Nations Environment Programme (UNEP) has called it one of the world's largest beach clean-ups in history.

Community spirit: As the months went on, more than 1,000 volunteers – including workers from local companies, school children and Bollywood stars – joined the clean-up project.

Now, after 21 <u>months of toil</u>, they have picked up 11,684,500 pounds of trash, most of it plastic, that had **accumulated** along the shoreline. They also cleaned 52 public toilets and planted 50 coconut trees.

For his vision and hard work, the UN awarded him the 'Champion of the Earth' award.

'I am an ocean lover and feel that we owe a duty to our ocean to make it free of plastic,' he told the UN. 'I just hope this is the beginning for <u>coastal communities</u> across India and the world.'

Shah's work didn't end with the last piece of trash picked up, either. He wants to plant thousands of coconut trees to return the beach to the **lagoon** it once was and he now works to limit the amount of garbage that makes it to the beach in the first place by, for example, building **barriers** along creeks upstream that carry litter to the beach.

He's also planning to expand his clean-up effort to the coastline's mangrove forests, which are similarly **infested** with garbage. When clean and **unobstructed**, these forests can act as powerful **filtration** systems and also form a natural defence against storms.

Shah also hopes to bring grassroots clean-up efforts to other parts of India, inspiring a nationwide awareness of environmentalism. Ultimately, Shah wants to export this **mentality** throughout the world, cleaning up oceans and **ecosystems** to create a world that can foster life in all its splendour.

It's going to be an uphill battle. Each year, 8 to 13 million tons of plastic make it into the world's oceans — the **equivalent** of two garbage trucks filled with plastic every minute. Throughout the world, there are about five plastic bags filled with plastic for every foot of coastline. By 2050, plastic could outweigh fish in the oceans.

While companies are to blame for the massive amounts of plastic produced and sold, plastic pollution often happens on an individual level. But if Shah's work proves anything, individuals can **transform** their relationship to garbage. Hopefully his style of enthusiastic environmentalism catches on around the world.

Evan's Response

Tom @tck15
Replying to @Evan
I'm gobsmacked! I can't get over the before and after pictures. Such a difference. Amazing teamwork! 👏

Evan @emk1
Replying to @Tom
Isn't it astounding how one person can make one big change? I wonder what the beach is like now. Community is so important. Must check out when our local Tidy Towns clean-up is on!

Tom @tck15
Replying to @Evan
Take a look at this report. It's in the *Guardian* – Headline: Mumbai Beach Goes From Dump to Turtle Hatchery in Two Years #beatplasticpollution #savetheanimals #environment

Evan @emk1
Replying to @Tom
Thanks, Tom! Next read sorted!

Author's Intent

Do you think the author wrote this to inform, persuade or entertain the reader?

What does the author want you to understand after you've finished reading the article?

Mrs World: A Global Warning
by Ros Asquith

Here's Mrs Volcano, vomiting ash,
   rumbling fire,
reciting a litany, Pompeii, Vesuvius,
   Montserrat.
Grrrrrrrrrrrrrrrrrrr.
Behind her Madam Desert, rippling,
   muscular,
her shifting sands dipping in search of
   oases.
Swisssssh.
And the great Queen Rainforest,
   shimmering, towering,
scattering luminous birds like loose
change.
The earth trembles.
Hush.

The Empress Water speaks:
'Almost all we have is I
and every year that trickles by
yet another droplet seeps
deep into my darkest deeps
Almost all we have is Me,
is river, ocean, lake and sea.
And yet I long and long to get
more and more, more wet, more wet.

And so I bid you, sisters all.
Sister Snowdrop, sweet and small,
Sister Ice-Cap, specially you,
here is all you have to do.
All your hopes have now gone west.
Why be bothered to protest?
Simply stand in line and wait,
drown your anger, slake your hate.

Instead, come make your peace
   with me,
come swim into my endless sea.
For you know you really oughta
be happy with your Sister Water.
Deserts will green beneath my waves
deep within these ocean caves.
Forests will be forever calm,
never more to suffer harm.
And even you, my Everest,
will sink into eternal rest.

For I can accommodate
humanity and all its hate.
Mankind will melt quite peacefully
deep within the sea of me.'

Writing to Socialise

Water

Carlos and Isabel's Intro

Hola, mis amigas! (Hello, my friends!)

This week we are taking a peek at **writing to socialise**. It's one of our favourite genres. There are many different ways of writing to socialise, including invitations, notes, greetings, memos, messages, postcards, emails and letters.

What's your favourite? We love writing postcards when we're on holiday. We always remind our friends to send us a postcard when they're on holiday too. We stick them on our fridge. Do any of you do that?

We have chosen some extracts from the start of the book *Regarding the Fountain: A Tale, in Letters, of Liars and Leaks* by Kate Klise. It's such a cool read. The story is told entirely through letters, notes, messages, postcards and telegraphs. We've never read anything like it before and definitely recommend you put it on your reading list.

Transfer of skills: Have you ever written a letter? In the past it was one of the main ways of communicating. Do you think it has become a lost art? Can you say the word 'letter' in another language? Do you notice any similarities?

litir (Irish), *list* (Polish), *carta* (Spanish), *lettera* (Italian)

Regarding the Fountain

Dry Creek Middle School
Dry Creek, Missouri
'We Thirst for Knowledge'

14 September

Mr Walter Russ
Principal

Flowing Waters Fountains, Etc.
Watertown, CA

Ms Waters:

Perhaps you misunderstood the letter written earlier this month by the secretary of our school.

As per my **request**, Ms Fisch wrote to you in the hopes of receiving information regarding a fountain. I am afraid, however, that she may not have made clear the nature of the fountain we are seeking.

While I'm sure the fountains you create for palaces and hotels are indeed lovely, we have no need for such **extravagance** in our school. Instead, what we are looking for is this:

Product:	drinking fountain
Style:	plain
Price:	**modest**

Would you please send the product description and price list of any fountains in your **inventory** that fit the above description?

Thank you for your time and **co-operation**.

Efficiently,

Walter Russ

Mr Walter Russ
Principal

Flowing Waters Fountains, Etc.

27 September

Dry Creek Middle School
Dry Creek, MO

Dear Mr Wally Russ,

I received your letter last week and, my goodness, you sound just like the author of the little book of directions that came with my blender.

I'm still not quite sure what your letter means (just as I'm not entirely certain how the blender works), but I'm guessing you'd like to see a **catalogue** of my fountains. Am I right? If so, I must repeat myself: I don't *have* a catalogue of my fountains. I never build the same fountain twice.

But here's my idea: Why don't I come to your school sometime in the next week or two? I'll make a few drawings in my sketchbook. I'll return to my workshop, begin **construction**, and bingo! Before you know it, you'll have yourself a new fountain.

What do you say, Wally?

Florence Waters

PS By the by, in the future, try not to blame your confusion on other people. Goldie Fisch made the request for a catalogue very clear the first time around.

DRY CREEK MIDDLE SCHOOL

M E M O

DATE: 1 OCTOBER

TO: GOLDIE FISCH

FR: PRINCIPAL WALTER RUSS

RE: THE FOUNTAIN

Ms Florence Waters will be visiting our school today.

As I will be in meetings all day, it will be your responsibility to show Ms Waters where the leaky drinking fountain is located. It seems she needs to 'see' the **destination** of her **product** before she can quote us a price on it.

You may need to impress upon her the fact that our desires regarding the fountain are purely functional. Dry Creek Middle School is neither a hotel nor a water park. Please remind Ms Waters of this.

Also, in her letter, Ms Waters addressed me as 'Wally'. Inform her that I prefer the unabbreviated version of 'Walter'.

Flowing Waters Fountains, Etc.

5 October

Dry Creek Middle School
Dry Creek, MO

Greetings, Goldie!

Thanks again for the wonderful tour of your school and town. What a <u>charming little hamlet</u>!

Oh yes, about the fountain. It should be fairly simple. Just a drinking fountain for the children, yes? That's easy enough. And it certainly won't take long to build.

There is one favour I would like to ask before I begin. A little teeny favour, actually.

Whenever I start a new fountain, I like to talk to the people who will see and use it once it's finished. It's important to me to hear what they think the fountain should look like.

In this case, I'd like to hear from the students in the classroom located right next to the fountain. The sign on the door said Mr Sam N's Fifth Graders. I knocked quietly, but no one answered the door. I guess they were out.

Goldie, would you do me the favour of giving my address to Mr Sam N and his students? Please ask them to send me their ideas for the fountain.

Thanks!
Your friend,

Flo Waters

PS I'm enclosing a sketch for you.

DATE: 9 October   HOUR: 9:20   TO: Sam N

WHILE YOU WERE OUT

Ms Florence Waters, President of Flowing Waters Fountains, Etc.

☐ Telephoned ☐ Returned Call ☐ Left Package ☐ Please Call ☒ Was In
☐ Please See Me ☐ Will Call Again ☒ Won't Call ☐ Important

MESSAGE: Florence Waters, the fountain <u>designer</u>, stopped by your classroom to speak to your students last week when you were all out on a <u>field trip</u>. No need to call her back (she doesn't have a phone), but she would like to hear your students' ideas regarding the fountain

SIGNED: Goldie F.

FIFTH GRADE ANNOUNCEMENTS

10 October

TODAY'S WRITING ASSIGNMENT:

As you all know, our school needs a new drinking fountain. A fountain designer by the name of Florence Waters has been asked to design it for us. Before she does, Ms Waters would like to hear what you think the new fountain should look like. Write a short paragraph or two describing your ideas for the perfect drinking fountain.

Because Ms Waters prefers to communicate* by letter, we will mail our ideas to her tomorrow.

Mr N

HISTORY CLUB MEETING: 3:30 TODAY

*WORD OF THE DAY: communicate. To interchange thoughts, feelings or ideas.

---

10 October

Dear Florence Waters,

Hello. My name is Tad Poll.

I'm very glad we're getting a new drinking fountain. The old one is awful!! It leaks all the time, so there's always a huge puddle around it. Blehh!!!

As long as you're building a new fountain, I think you should make it different (and better) than the old boring (and leaky) kind. Can you make it so that the water comes out in a loop-the-loop? I'll draw a picture to show you what I mean.

Sincerely,

Tad

10/10

Hi, Ms Waters!

We wish the new fountain could be big enough so that we could splash around it **between classes.**

Love,

Lily and Paddy

10 October

Dear Ms Waters,

I am in 5th grade. I am writing to you about the fountain.

Once when I was on **vacation**, I saw a glass-bottomed boat. It was like a regular boat, only it had glass in the bottom so you could look down and see all the fish in the water.

Do you think maybe you could do this with the fountain at our school? Instead of glass-bottomed, make it a glass-sided fountain. That way, we could put fish in our fountain. It would be like an aquarium and a drinking fountain all in one.

I like fish. Last year I did a report on tropical fish for science fair. Goldie Fisch let me use her aquarium.

Yours truly,

Minnie O

---

10 October

Dear Fountain Designer,

When you build the fountain for our school, do you think it would be possible to have other things come out of it besides just water?

Maybe there could be different buttons for things like lemonade, chocolate milk and root beer. (Maybe even chocolate shakes????)

Yours truly,

Shelly and Gil

PS Fifth graders rule!!

---

10 October

Dear Ms Waters,

My students have enjoyed using their imaginations to design the perfect drinking fountain. I like Lily and Paddy's idea of making the drinking fountain big enough to splash around in between classes. While you're at it, maybe you can add a hot tub and a whirlpool for the teachers to splash around in after school.

Hey, a teacher can dream, can't he?

With kind regards,

Mr Sam N

Fifth-grade teacher

Carlos and Isabel's Response

Does your school have a drinking fountain? Wouldn't it be so cool if every school had one?

Poll Who thinks that every school should have a drinking fountain?

We thought Shelly and Gil's letter was brilliant. We would definitely agree with having different buttons for things like chocolate milk! We love chocolate. Who doesn't? If you could have three buttons on the fountain, what would they be for?

I hope you enjoyed this extract. Did you have a favourite letter or note? And guess what? We still have another extract to go on writing to socialise. You will be an expert on letter writing in no time!

Author's Intent

I wonder what inspired Kate Klise to write such a book.

I think she definitely has thought outside the box! Do you agree or disagree?

Do you think she is trying to inform, persuade or entertain us?

The Drinking Fountain
by Kenn Nesbitt

The drinking fountain squirted me.
It shot right up my nose.
It felt as if I'd stuck my nostril
on the garden hose.

It squirted water in my eye
and also in my ear.
I'm having trouble seeing
and it's really hard to hear.

The water squirted east and west.
It squirted north and south.
Upon my shirt, my pants, my hair,
but nothing in my mouth.

I'm sure that soon they'll fix it
but, until then, let me think …
just whom can I convince that they
should come and have a drink?

Writing to Socialise

Hallowe'en

Alex's Intro

Dia daoibh, a chairde, conas atá sibh? Oíche Shamhna Shona Daoibh! (Hello, friends. How are you? Happy Hallowe'en!) This is one of my favourite times of year. There's always so much to do: carving pumpkins, decorating our house as a spooky lair, dressing up, watching Hallowe'en movies … Are you excited?

> Before you finish up for the midterm break, we are going to look at one more extract in the genre of **writing to socialise**. Can you remember all the different ways of writing to socialise?

We are going to read extracts from *Dying to Meet You: 43 Old Cemetery Road* by Kate Klise. It will get us into the Hallowe'en spirit!

Transfer of skills: Haunted houses can be scary places. However, is it our imagination that tricks us into thinking they're haunted? Can you say 'haunted house' in another language? Let's take a look.

teach taibhsí (Irish), *kummitus talo* (Finnish), *spookhuis* (Dutch), *hemsökt hus* (Swedish)

> **My reading goal** ★ Vary my tone and use pitch to express the mood of the characters.

Dying to Meet You

IGNATIUS B. GRUMPLY

SPECIALISING IN MYSTERIES, MAYHEM & THE MACABRE
TEMPORARY ADDRESS

43 OLD CEMETERY ROAD   GHASTLY, ILLINOIS

20 June

Ms Anita Sale
Proper Properties
100 Larkin Street
San Francisco, CA 94102

Ms Sale:

It is one thing to provide summer babysitting services for an **abandoned** child. It is quite another to do so for a child who suffers from **hallucinations** and/or is a shameless liar.

I am referring to Seymour Hope, who has informed me that a 'ghost' named Olive is living in the cupola of this house, and cooking for him and his cat on a nightly basis.

Now, I am well aware that children have a strange fascination with the **macabre**. I have made (and lost) a fortune due to this very fact.

But Ms Sale, this Hope boy is stomping around in the cupola, slamming doors, stealing library books *and* banging on a tuneless piano at midnight, thereby distracting me from writing my next book, which is why I rented this so-called Victorian lady in the first place.

If you won't refund my rent, you can at least tell me how and where to contact the boy's parents. Their son clearly needs professional help. I intend to inform them of such, if you will promptly send me their summer address.

Responsibly,

I. B. Grumply

I. B. Grumply

PROPER PROPERTIES

Elegant Estates   Historic Homes   **Classic Cottages**

100 Larkin Street
San Francisco, CA 94102

23 June

Mr Ignatius B. Grumply
43 Old Cemetery Road
Ghastly, Illinois

Dear Mr Grumply,

I do have an address for Les and Diane Hope. In fact, I am the only person who knows where they are during their lecture tour. But I'm afraid I can't share that information with you. I'm under <u>strict orders</u> *not* to contact them unless I have a buyer for their house.

Regarding Seymour: I'm afraid I know *all* about him. That boy has successfully scared away every **prospective** renter *and* buyer I've found for Spence Mansion with his 'ghost' stories and **imitations**. He even wrote me a letter last month, telling me how he planned to buy the house himself. 'I happen to like living here with Olive,' Seymour wrote. 'I'm the only person who can see her, but only when she *wants* to be seen, which isn't all that often. Olive likes her privacy. And she doesn't like people who try to make money off her, like my parents wanted to do.'

Of course Seymour needs professional help. But I'm afraid I can't share his parents' summer address with you – unless *you're* interested in buying Spence Mansion. If so, I'd be happy to put you in touch with Les and Diane Hope!

If it's any comfort, there's no need to worry about a ghost in Spence Mansion. Les and Diane Hope are world-famous professors of the **paranormal**. They bought the house at 43 Old Cemetery Road actually *hoping* to find a ghost but couldn't. What they discovered instead was that their son was even more **delusional** than they thought.

Now can you understand why Professors Les and Diane Hope didn't want their son to go to Europe with them? He's a very sick boy, and his <u>silly shenanigans</u> threaten to **undermine** his parents' research findings – not to mention *my* ability to sell Spence Mansion.

Sincerely,

Anita $ale

Anita Sale

PS How's the book coming along? I hope it's not unlucky to write the 13th book in a series.

IGNATIUS B. GRUMPLY

SPECIALISING IN MYSTERIES, MAYHEM & THE MACABRE
TEMPORARY ADDRESS

43 OLD CEMETERY ROAD   GHASTLY, ILLINOIS

26 June

Ms Anita Sale
Proper Properties
100 Larkin Street
San Francisco, CA 94102

Ms Sale:

Me – interested in buying this old rattrap? I hardly think so.

Nor am I frightened by schoolyard rumours and/or cheap imitations of ghosts. Why? For the simple reason, Ms Sale, that there are *no such things as ghosts*.

Your staggering unwillingness to be of assistance is matched only by your <u>stultifying ignorance</u>.

I. B. Grumply

I. B. Grumply

PS Only <u>illiterate imbeciles</u> such as yourself believe in black magic and unlucky numbers. For your information, and despite the **abysmal** conditions under which I am working, the book is coming along just fine. I shall **resume** my work on it as soon as I post this letter.

<u>Book #13 in the Ghost Tamer series</u>

Mystery at Old Cemetery Road: Bartholomew Brown Returns!

Chapter One

The house was old and creaky. Had he known exactly how old and creaky, Bartholomew Brown would never have rented it for the summer.

But rent it he had. And so, the famous ghost detective proposed to make the best of it.

He decided the situation called for a nice meal in a <u>fine dining</u> establishment. He hadn't eaten since very early in the day, and his appetite was keen. Nobody relished the anticipation of a good meal like Bartholomew Brown.

But just as he reached for his hat and linen jacket, a mongrel cat crept in his room with a baked chicken thigh, dripping with cream sauce, dangling from its feral jaws.

Bartholomew Brown's appetite evaporated.

'This,' he sighed, 'could be a very long summer.'

O.C.S.

Thursday, 26 June

My sentiments exactly.

But it's still boring. Your book, I mean. I read it while you were taking a walk.

Olive

IGNATIUS B. GRUMPLY

SPECIALISING IN MYSTERIES, MAYHEM & THE MACABRE
TEMPORARY ADDRESS

43 OLD CEMETERY ROAD

GHASTLY, ILLINOIS

26 June

Seymour Hope
Third Floor
43 Old Cemetery Road
Ghastly, Illinois

Seymour:

You little twit. How dare you call my work in progress *boring*? And what were you doing in my room?

If you continue to **violate** the established house rules, I shall have to punish you.

Oh, very clever. Slamming doors again, are we? While playing the piano. I believe I know a young boy who needs a spanking.

On my way to the third floor,

I. B. Grumply

I. B. Grumply

O.C.S.

Thursday, 26 June

If you lay one hand on that boy, you will regret it.

Olive

Greater Ghastly Memorial Hospital

4 Morgue Way
Ghastly, Illinois

1 July

E. Gadds
Attorney-at-Law
188 Madison Avenue
New York, NY 10016

Gadds:

I'm writing this from the hospital. Don't worry. The emergency has passed and I am still alive, if somewhat shaken.

It was the strangest thing. On Thursday night of last week at approximately seven o'clock, I was marching down the second-floor hallway on my way to talk some sense, in the form of a spanking, into my 11-year-old housemate, when a crystal chandelier came crashing down from the ceiling.

It missed me – but only by a matter of inches. I couldn't avoid stepping on several **shards** of glass, which punctured my Italian slippers.

Hence the four stitches in my left foot and six stitches in my right.

But here's the oddest part: Minutes before this happened, the boy, who's still trying to scare me with his 'ghost' imitations, slipped a note under my door, telling me that I would regret laying as much as one hand on him.

That is, I *think* it was the boy. I didn't actually see him slip the note under my door – or even write it, for that matter. If I didn't know better, I might think …

Never mind. This whole situation is completely preposterous. And yes, I intend to weave it *all* into the book, if I can just get a little peace and quiet so I can *write*.

No need to respond to this letter, Gadds. I just needed someone to talk to. I feel better already.

I shall be back at work on the book as soon as I'm released from the hospital.

With confidence and only a slight limp,

Ignatius

Ignatius B. Grumply

---

2 July

Hi, Olive!

Nice job getting rid of Mr Grumply.

– Seymour

Alex's Response

What do you think of my poem?

Hope boy tells Mr Grumply there's a ghost,

And what do you believe?

Lies or truth, what do you think?

Like it or not, the facts are the facts.

Out of nowhere a crystal chandelier came crashing down

With a big BANG!

Embedded in glass.

Eerily receiving a note under the door,

Now was it the boy or the ghost?

Did you enjoy the extract? I sure did! I can't wait to see what Olive will do next. What do you think she might get up to? Why do you think the author decided to write a book based around a haunted house? Do you like writing Hallowe'en stories?

Hope everyone has an awesome Hallowe'en!

Author's Intent

How is this extract similar to the one in the last unit?

What do you think of the author's choice of title? Do you think it's a good one? Why do you think that?

The Ghost Teacher
by Allan Ahlberg

The school is closed, the children gone,
But the ghost of a teacher lingers on.
As the daylight fades, as the daytime ends,
As the night draws in and the dark descends,
She stands in the classroom, as clear as glass.
And calls the names of her absent class.

The school is shut, the children grown,
But the ghost of the teacher, all alone,
Puts the date on the board and moves about
(As the night draws on and the stars come out)
Between the desks – a glow in the gloom –
And calls for quiet in the silent room.

The school is a ruin, the children fled,
But the ghost of the teacher, long-time dead,
As the moon comes up and the first owls glide,
Puts on her coat and steps outside.
In the moonlit playground, shadow-free,
She stands on duty with a cup of tea.

The school is forgotten – children forget –
But the ghost of a teacher lingers yet.
As the night creeps up to the edge of the day,
She tidies the Plasticine away;
Counts the scissors – a shimmer of glass –
And says, 'Off you go!' to her absent class.

She utters the words that no one hears,
Picks up her bag ...
                and
                        disappears.

Narrative

At School

Lainey's Intro

Hello, everyone! I've set myself a challenge this year — to read 50 BOOKS! What a goal! Luckily enough, we have an amazing library and a super librarian who is great at recommending books.

I just finished reading *Wonder* by R.J. Palacio. Have you read it? If not, you definitely have to put it on your reading bucket list. I couldn't stop talking about it and wanted to read something similar, so the librarian recommended *Out of My Mind* by Sharon Draper. I'm already on Chapter 11.

This week we'll be reading a **narrative** text. These texts are written to engage and entertain the reader. I'll fill you in on some of the features, with examples from the book that we're going to read from:

- **Characters:** Melody, Melody's parents, Melody's sister Penny, Mrs V.
- **Setting:** Melody's home, school and classroom.
- **Plot:** Melody is an 11-year-old child who is wheelchair bound due to her cerebral palsy. This is her journey through fifth grade.
- **Problem:** Melody finds it extremely hard to communicate and make friends.
- **Solution:** I haven't got that far yet!
- **Theme:** I have a few ideas. Check in after this chapter to see if I was right!

Transfer of skills: This text takes place in a school setting. Can you say the word 'school' in another language? Let's take a look.

scoil (Irish), *szkoła* (Polish), *colegio* (Spanish), *école* (French)

> **My reading goal** ★ Pay attention to commas – pause for a breath, then read on.

Out of My Mind

<u>Fifth grade</u> started a few weeks ago, and a couple of cool things have happened. Well, I didn't get a gadget that makes Garfield-like speech bubbles over my head, but I did get an electric wheelchair, and our school began something called '<u>inclusion classes</u>'. I thought that was funny. I've never been included in anything. But these classes are supposed to give kids like me a chance to interact with what everybody else calls the 'normal' students. What's normal?! Duh!

Comparing my new chair to my old one is like comparing a Mercedes to a skateboard. The wheels are almost like car tires, which makes the ride smooth and easy, like riding on pillows. I can't go very fast, but can **propel** myself down the hall with just a little lever on the handrail. Or, if I flip the switch to **manual**, I can still be pushed if necessary.

When Freddy first saw it, he shouted, 'Woo-hoo!' like I'd just won the Indy 500. 'Melly go zoom zoom now! Wanna race?' He spun his own chair in excited circles around me.

I'm sure he could beat me, even at the <u>subatomic speeds</u> our chairs are set to.

My electric chair is a lot heavier than my manual chair, and it's almost impossible for Mom and Dad to lift anywhere. 'When you decide to switch to a rocket ship for transportation,' Dad joked at first, rubbing his back, 'you're gonna need to hire Superman to get it in the car!'

I grinned. But I know he saw the thanks in my eyes.

So he bought a set of <u>portable wheelchair ramps</u> that fold and fit in the back of our SUV. With those, he can roll the new chair into the back of our car and still have back muscles left over.

For me, it's all about the freedom. Now I don't have to wait for somebody to move me across the room. I can just go there. Nice. So when they decided to start **mainstreaming** us into the regular classes, the electric chair was really helpful.

Our fifth-grade teacher in room H-5 reminds me of a television grandmother. Mrs Shannon is **pudgy**, wears lavender body lotion every single day, and I think she must be from the South because she talks with a <u>real strong drawl</u>. Somehow it makes everything she says seem more interesting.

She told us on the first day, 'I'm gonna bust a gut makin' sure y'all get all you can out of this school year, you hear? We're gonna read, and learn, and grow. I believe every one of y'all got **potential** all stuffed inside, and together we're gonna try to make some of that stuff shine.'

I liked her. She brought in stacks of new books to read to us, as well as games and music and videos. Unlike Mrs Billups, Mrs Shannon must have read all our records because she dusted off the headphones and even brought in more books on tape for me.

'Ya'll ready for music class?' she asked us one morning. 'Let's get this inclusion stuff goin'!'

I <u>jerked with excitement</u>. As the aides helped us down the hall to the music room, I wondered if I'd get to sit next to a regular kid. What if I did something stupid? What if Willy yodelled, or Carl farted? Maria was likely to blurt out something crazy. Would this be our only chance? What if we messed this up? I could barely contain myself. We are going to be in a *regular* classroom!

The music teacher, Mrs Lovelace, had been the first to volunteer to open her class to us. The music room was huge – almost twice as large as our classroom. My hands got sweaty.

The kids in there were mostly fifth graders too. They'd probably be surprised to know that I knew all their names. I've watched them on the playground, at lunch and at **recess** for years. My classmates sit under a tree and catch a breeze while they play kickball or tag, so I know who they are and how they work. I doubted if they knew any of *us* by name, though.

Well, the whole thing was almost a disaster. Willy, probably upset and scared about being in a new room, started yelping at the top of his lungs. Jill began to cry. She held tightly to the hand grips of her walker and refused to move past the doorway. I wanted to disappear.

All of the 'normal' children in the music class – I guess about thirty of them – turned to stare. Some of them laughed. Others looked away. But one girl in the back row crossed her arms across her chest and **scowled** at her classmates who were acting up.

Two girls, Molly and Claire – everyone knew them because they were mean to almost everybody on the playground – **mimicked** Willy. They made sure they stayed just out of the teacher's line of sight. But I saw it. So did Willy.

'Hey, Claire!' Molly said, twisting her arms above her head and bending her body so it looked crooked. 'Look at me! I'm a retard!' She laughed so hard, she snorted snot.

Claire cracked up as well, then let spit dribble out of her mouth. 'Duh buh wuh buh,' she said, crossing her eyes and pretending to slip out of her chair. Mrs Lovelace finally noticed them, because she said **sternly**, 'Stand up please, Claire.'

'I didn't do anything!' Claire replied.

'You stand as well, Molly,' Mrs Lovelace added.

'We were just laughing,' Molly said **defensively**. But she stood up next to Claire.

Mrs Lovelace took both girls' chairs and slid them over to the wall.

'Why'd you do that?' Claire cried out in protest.

'You have perfectly good bodies and legs that work. Use them,' Mrs Lovelace instructed.

'You can't make us stand the whole class!' Claire moaned.

'The board of education requires that I teach you music. There is nothing in the rule book that requires you to sit down while I do it. Now stand there and be quiet, or I'll send you to the office for showing disrespect to our guests.'

They stood. In the middle of the third row of chairs, where everyone else was seated comfortably, they stood.

This teacher is awesome!

After that, things went more smoothly. Jill, who had continued to cry, had been taken back to our room by one of the **aides**. The rest of us sat quietly in the back of the room.

Mrs Lovelace began class once more. 'I think we need a moment to gather ourselves, children.' She sat down at her piano and began to play 'Moon River', and then she switched to the theme song from one of those new vampire movies. Oh, yeah, she knew what we liked. When I started seeing the colours, I knew she was good. Forest green, lime green, emerald.

I glanced over at Gloria. Instead of sitting all curled up like she usually did, her arms were outstretched like she was trying to catch the music and bring it to her. Her face was almost glowing. She began to sway with the music.

Then Mrs Lovelace completely changed tempo and played the opening notes to 'Take Me Out to the Ball Game'. Willy clapped his hands wildly.

Finally, the teacher started to play 'Boogie Woogie Bugle Boy'. Dad would have loved it. Kids started to shimmy in their seats. Maria got up and started dancing! She clapped loudly, never quite on the beat, but to a rhythm that was all her own.

Mrs Lovelace paused at the end of the song. 'Music is powerful, my young friends,' she said. 'It can connect us to memories. It can influence our mood and our responses to problems we might face.'

<u>She cut her eyes</u> at Claire and Molly, who still stood in the empty places where their chairs had been.

I wanted to tell Mrs Lovelace I liked music too. I wanted to know if she'd ever heard the song 'Elvira' or if she would teach us how to make our own music. I tried to raise my hand, but she didn't notice me. It must have looked like just another one of those random movements that kids like me seem to make. But I had the feeling that Mrs Lovelace was someone who'd take the time to figure me out.

The teacher went on. 'Before I continue with the lesson, let's make this a real inclusion experience. Perhaps our friends from room H-5 would like to sit with the rest of us instead of being stuck in the back.'

Freddy heard that and took his chance. He put his chair into gear and zoomed to the front of that big room and shouted, 'I am Freddy. I like music. I go fast!'

The class laughed. I can tell the difference between people making fun of us and people being nice to us. Freddy could too, so he joined in the laughter. Mrs Lovelace looked momentarily **startled**, then went over to Freddy, shook his hand, and welcomed him to the class. She sat him right there in front, next to a boy named Rodney. Rodney gave Freddy a high five, and the two of them grinned at each other. Okay, I had to admit it – I was jealous.

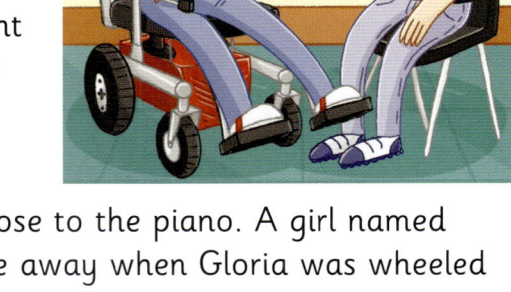

Mrs Lovelace asked an aide to bring Gloria down front close to the piano. A girl named Elizabeth glanced at Gloria nervously, but she didn't move away when Gloria was wheeled next to her.

Elizabeth's best friend is a girl named Jessica. At recess they sit together near the fence and share granola bars. I've always wondered what they whisper about. I also noticed that everything Elizabeth does, Jessica tries to outdo. Like, if Elizabeth beats her running to the fence, Jessica insists they run again so she can win too. Or if Elizabeth gets a new book bag, Jessica will have a new one the next day.

So when Elizabeth started talking to Gloria, who looked terrified, Jessica raised her hand and asked if one of the H-5 kids could sit next to her.

Maria might have trouble figuring out some stuff, but she's a real friendly person. 'I wanna sit by the blue-shirt girl. I wanna sit by the blue-shirt girl,' she demanded. She stomped down to Jessica's seat and sat down next to her. Then she jumped back up and gave Jessica a hug, then gave a hug to the kids sitting closest to Jessica. One kid stiffened up when she touched him, but I was surprised that most of them let her hug them. Molly and Claire, since they were standing, had no choice.

'Ooh, yuck!' Claire whispered.

'Cooties!' Molly whispered back.

Mrs Lovelace raised an eyebrow, then cleared her throat. 'It seems you two like to stand. You'll continue to do so the rest of this week.'

'Aw man! This sucks!' I heard Claire say.

Molly had sense enough to say nothing.

Maria didn't notice. She even kissed Claire on the cheek. That was funny.

Willy ended up next to a large, friendly boy named Connor.

Ashley and Carl were absent that day, so that left me sitting in the back of the classroom by myself. The room got real quiet. I suddenly felt cold, like the air-conditioning had been <u>cranked up</u> real high. I got goose bumps.

The teacher looked around the room, expectation on her face, I guess hoping that somebody would volunteer to take me. At that moment I would have given anything to be back in our bluebird room instead of sitting there with thirty kids staring at me.

LAINEY'S RESPONSE

Wow! A totally awesome recommendation from the librarian. This chapter introduced us to new characters and it really gave me great insight into Melody's life in school. I can't believe how Claire and Molly are acting, can you? I think they are horrible characters. I wonder who will sit with Melody. I can well imagine that she wants to be back in the bluebird room. It must seem like an eternity waiting for someone to volunteer.

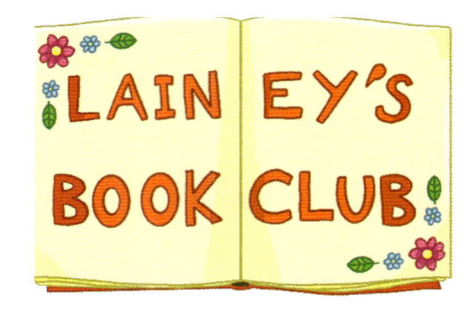

Let's take a look at our features again and fill them in:

- **Characters:** Mrs Shannon, Mrs Lovelace, Freddy, Rodney, Maria, Willy, Claire, Molly, Gloria, Elizabeth, Jessica, Connor.
- **Setting:** Room H-5 (the bluebird room) and music class.
- **Plot:** Melody joins an inclusion class in the subject of music.
- **Problem:** Some of the children's reactions to the inclusion of students from H-5.
- **Solution:** I'm still working on this one!
- **Theme:** I'm thinking that a main theme could be respect – that everyone has the right to be respected. What are your ideas?

AUTHOR'S INTENT

What do you think the author hoped to accomplish by writing this story? Did she hope to entertain, to arouse empathy, to prove something or to state facts?

> What do you think? Are you eager to read on? If so, check if your local library or bookshop has the book in stock. I can't wait to finish it. I wonder what inspired Sharon Draper to write a novel like this.

Different

by Ros Asquith

I want to be wild as a caged bird.
I want to be dark as the light.
I must sing like a fish, I must weep like a stone.
I want to be bright as the night.

I want to be heavy as feathers
And to float on the ocean like lead.
To be quiet as thunder and fierce as a lamb
And never to sleep in a bed.

I want to run faster than lamp posts.
I want to be dry, like the sea.
To fly like a flower, to flame like the ice.
I want to be free to be me.

Narrative

Adventure

Meg and Mel's Intro

Welcome to our pick of the week: *The Lion, the Witch and the Wardrobe*.

We are reading a **narrative** text this week. The purpose of narrative texts is to tell stories. They are written to entertain and engage the reader in an imaginary experience.

Here are the narrative features that we should be on the lookout for:
- **Characters:** The people or animals in the story.
- **Setting:** Where the story takes place.
- **Plot:** This is what happens in the story. It is the sequence of events.
- **Problem:** The obstacles, struggles or conflicts the characters face.
- **Solution:** The way the characters solve the problem.
- **Theme:** The main idea of the story or the message or lesson the author wants you to learn.

Narratives are our favourite text to read. We love being able to follow characters on their adventures.

We chose this text because we know *The Lion, the Witch and the Wardrobe* is a classic book. A classic book is noted as being exemplary. It definitely should be worth the read. Can you name any other classic books? In this book there are four children: Lucy, Peter, Susan and Edmund. They open a door and enter a magical world. What could the magical world be like? Check out our review at the end!

Transfer of skills: Reading can transport us to other worlds. Have you ever read a book that took you into another world? Do you know what the word 'book' is in another language? Do you notice any similarities?

leabhar (Irish), *libro* (Spanish), *livre* (French), *bok* (Swedish), *buch* (German)

> **My reading goal** ★ Examine how speech marks are used and how question marks affect the tone of voice.

The Lion, the Witch and the Wardrobe

> This novel was written by C.S. Lewis. It was first published in 1950. It took 10 years to write. It is Book 2 in the classic fantasy series *The Chronicles of Narnia*. This book has been made into a film. The film was released in 2005 and earned more than $745 million worldwide. Let's see where it all started …

Chapter 1 – Lucy Looks into a Wardrobe

Once there were four children whose names were Peter, Susan, Edmund and Lucy. This story is about something that happened to them when they were sent away from London during the war because of the **air-raids**. They were sent to the house of an old Professor who lived in the heart of the country, ten miles from the nearest railway station and two miles from the nearest post office. He had no wife and he lived in a very large house with a housekeeper called Mrs Macready and three servants. (Their names were Ivy, Margaret and Betty, but they do not come into the story much.) He himself was a very old man with shaggy white hair which grew over most of his face as well as on his head, and they liked him almost at once; but on the first evening when he came out to meet them at the front door he was so odd-looking that Lucy (who was the youngest) was a little afraid of him, and Edmund (who was the next youngest) wanted to laugh and had to keep on pretending to blow his nose to hide it.

As soon as they had said goodnight to the Professor and gone upstairs on the first night, the boys came into the girls' room and they all talked it over.

'We've fallen on our feet and no mistake,' said Peter. 'This is going to be perfectly **splendid**. That old chap will let us do anything we like.'

'I think he's an old dear,' said Susan.

'Oh, come off it!' said Edmund, who was tired and pretending not to be tired, which always made him bad-tempered. 'Don't go on talking like that.'

'Like what?' said Susan; 'and anyway, it's time you were in bed.'

'Trying to talk like Mother,' said Edmund. 'And who are you to say when I'm to go to bed? Go to bed yourself.'

'Hadn't we all better go to bed?' said Lucy.

'There's sure to be a row if we're heard talking here.'

'No there won't,' said Peter. 'I tell you this is the sort of house where no one's going to mind what we do. Anyway, they won't hear us. It's about ten minutes' walk from here down to that dining room, and any amount of stairs and passages in between.'

'What's that noise?' said Lucy suddenly. It was a far larger house than she had ever been in before and the thought of all those long passages and rows of doors leading into empty rooms was beginning to make her feel a little creepy.

'It's only a bird, silly,' said Edmund.

'It's an owl,' said Peter. 'This is going to be a wonderful place for birds. I shall go to bed now. I say, let's go and explore tomorrow. You might find anything in a place like this. Did you see those mountains as we came along? And the woods? There might be eagles. There might be stags. There'll be hawks.'

'Badgers!' said Lucy.

'Foxes!' said Edmund.

'Rabbits!' said Susan.

But when the next morning came there was a steady rain falling, so thick that when you looked out of the window you could see neither the mountains nor the woods nor even the stream in the garden.

'Of course it *would* be raining!' said Edmund. They had just finished their breakfast with the Professor and were upstairs in the room he had set apart for them – a long, low room with two windows looking out in one direction and two in another.

'Do stop grumbling, Ed,' said Susan. '<u>Ten to one</u> it'll clear up in an hour or so. And in the meantime we're pretty well off. There's a **wireless** and lots of books.'

'Not for me,' said Peter; 'I'm going to explore in the house.'

Everyone agreed to this and that was how the adventures began. It was the sort of house that you never seem to come to the end of, and it was full of unexpected places. The first few doors they tried led only into spare bedrooms, as everyone had expected that they would; but soon they came to a very long room full of pictures, and there they found a suit of armour; and after that was a room all hung with green, with a harp in one corner; and then came three steps down and five steps up, and then a kind of little upstairs hall and a door that led out on to a balcony, and then a whole series of rooms that led into each other and were lined with books – most of them very old books and some bigger than a Bible in a church. And shortly after that they looked into a room that was quite empty except for one big wardrobe; the sort that has a **looking-glass** in the door. There was nothing else in the room at all except a dead **bluebottle** on the window-sill.

'Nothing there!' said Peter, and they all trooped out again – all except Lucy. She stayed behind because she thought it would be worthwhile trying the door of the wardrobe, even though she felt almost sure that it would be locked. To her surprise it opened quite easily, and two **mothballs** dropped out.

Looking into the inside, she saw several coats hanging up – mostly long fur coats. There was nothing Lucy liked so much as the smell and feel of fur. She **immediately** stepped into the wardrobe and got in among the coats and rubbed her face against them, leaving the door open, of course, because she knew that it is very foolish to shut oneself into any wardrobe. Soon she went in further and found that there was a second row of coats hanging up behind the first one. It was almost quite dark in there and she kept her arms stretched out in front of her so as not to bump her face into the back of the wardrobe. She took a step further in – then two or three steps – always expecting to feel woodwork against the tips of her fingers. But she could not feel it.

'This must be a simply **enormous** wardrobe,' thought Lucy, going still further in and pushing the soft folds of the coats aside to make room for her. Then she noticed that there was something crunching under her feet. 'I wonder is that more mothballs?' she thought, stooping down to feel it with her hand. But instead of feeling the hard, smooth wood of the floor of the wardrobe, she felt something soft and powdery and extremely cold. 'This is very queer,' she said, and went on a step or two further.

Next moment she found that what she was rubbing against her face and hands was no longer soft fur but something hard and rough and even prickly. 'Why, it is just like branches of trees!' exclaimed Lucy. And then she saw that there was a light ahead of her; not a few inches away where the back of the wardrobe ought to have been, but a long way off. Something cold and soft was falling on her. A moment later she found that she was standing in the middle of a wood at night-time with snow under her feet and snowflakes falling through the air.

Lucy felt a little frightened, but she felt very **inquisitive** and excited as well. She looked back over her shoulder and there, between the dark tree-trunks, she could still see the open doorway of the wardrobe and even catch a glimpse of the empty room from which she had set out. (She had, of course, left the door open, for she knew that it is a very silly thing to shut oneself into a wardrobe.) It seemed to be still daylight there. 'I can always get back if anything goes wrong,' thought Lucy. She began to walk forward, *crunch-crunch* over the snow and through the wood towards the other light.

In about ten minutes she reached it and found it was a lamp-post. As she stood looking at it, wondering why there was a lamp-post in the middle of the wood and wondering what to do next, she heard a pitter patter of feet coming towards her. And soon after that a very strange person stepped out from the trees into the light of the lamp-post.

He was only a little taller than Lucy herself and he carried over his head an umbrella, white with snow. From the waist upwards he was like a man, but his legs were shaped like a goat's (the hair on them was glossy black) and instead of feet he had goat's hoofs. He also had a tail, but Lucy did not notice this at first because it was neatly caught up over the arm that held the umbrella so as to keep it from trailing in the snow. He had a red woollen **muffler** round his neck, and his skin was rather reddish too. He had a strange, but pleasant little face, with a short pointed beard and curly hair, and out of the hair stuck two horns, one on each side of his forehead. One of his hands, as I have said, held the umbrella; in the other arm he carried several brown paper **parcels**. What with the parcels and the snow it looked just as if had been doing his Christmas shopping. He was a Faun. And when he saw Lucy he gave such a start of surprise that he dropped all his parcels.

'<u>Goodness gracious</u> me!' exclaimed the Faun.

Chapter 2 – What Lucy Found There

'Good evening,' said Lucy. But the Faun was so busy picking up its parcels that at first it did not reply. When it had finished, it made her a little bow.

'Good evening, good evening,' said the Faun. 'Excuse me – I don't want to be inquisitive – but should I be right in thinking that you are a Daughter of Eve?'

'My name's Lucy,' said she, not quite understanding him.

'But you are – forgive me – you are what they call a girl?' said the Faun.

'Of course I'm a girl,' said Lucy.

'You are in fact Human?'

'Of course I'm human,' said Lucy, still a little puzzled.

'To be sure, to be sure,' said the Faun. 'How stupid of me! But I've never seen a Son of Adam or a Daughter of Eve before. I am delighted. That is to say—' and then it stopped as if it had been going to say something it had not **intended** but had remembered in time. 'Delighted, delighted,' he went on. 'Allow me to introduce myself. My name is Tumnus.'

'I am very pleased to meet you, Mr Tumnus,' said Lucy.

'And may I ask, O Lucy Daughter of Eve,' said Mr Tumnus, 'how you have come into Narnia?'

'Narnia? What's that?' said Lucy.

'This is the land of Narnia,' said the Faun.

MEG AND MEL'S RESPONSE

Title: *The Lion, the Witch and the Wardrobe*
Author: C.S. Lewis
Characters:
- Peter
- Susan
- Edmund
- Lucy
- The Professor
- The Faun

Plot: Peter, Susan, Edmund and Lucy have been sent to live in the countryside with a professor. On their first day it is pouring rain, so they decide to explore the house. They discover a room with a large wardrobe. Lucy steps inside and arrives in Narnia, where she meets a 'faun'.

Would you recommend this book to a friend?

We definitely would recommend this book to a friend. We're hooked already!

We are immediately introduced to the characters: the Professor, the four siblings and the Faun. We are given insight into the siblings' personalities through their reactions to the Professor, their dialogue with each other and their exploration of the house.

Through the author's descriptive writing, we see that the story is set in the countryside in a big house. The Professor's house sounds amazing – it is full of interesting rooms with unusual objects. We would love to play hide-and-seek in it!

We can connect this to the Harry Potter books. Harry uses a magical doorway through the platform 9¾. Lucy uses the magical doorway through the wardrobe.

We wonder if Lucy will be able to trust the Faun. Do Lucy's brothers and sister realise she has gone? We wonder what inspired the author to write this story. Did he live in a big house like the Professor's? Why did it take him 10 years to write the book?

AUTHOR'S INTENT

What was the author's purpose in writing this text?

What pictures does the author paint for the reader? How does he achieve this?

> Well, the author has certainly captured our attention! We can't wait to find out what happens to Lucy. We'll definitely be downloading this on our Kindles!

The Door

by Miroslav Holub

Go and open the door.
Maybe outside there's
a tree, or a wood,
a garden,
or a magic city.

Go and open the door.
Maybe a dog's rummaging.
Maybe you'll see a face,
or an eye,
or the picture
of a picture.

Go and open the door.
If there's a fog
it will clear.

Go and open the door.
Even if there's only
the darkness ticking,
even if there's only
the hollow wind,
even if
nothing
is there,
go and open the door.

At least
there'll be
a draught.

Narrative

Legends

Carlos and Isabel's Intro

Hola, mis amigas. ¿Qué pasa? (Hello, my friends. How are things?) It's our turn to present a book talk in class, so we have been busy researching.

Do you know what a book talk is? It's a short presentation about a book. We have to convince others to read it. We then put the book in our Book Talk Basket, and if someone wants to read it they sign their name to check it out of the basket. Our task was to pick a book from the genre of **narrative**.

We're thinking of picking *Where the Mountain Meets the Moon* by Grace Lin. Check out the reviews and the extract. We will check in afterwards to see what you

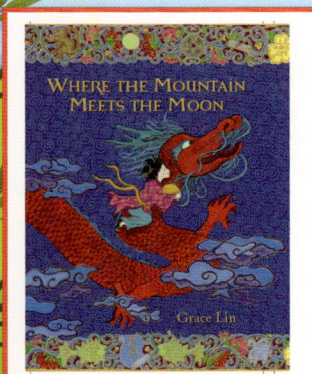

Where the Mountain Meets the Moon

Age:	11+
Author:	Grace Lin
Published:	2009
Genre:	Narrative – Fantasy
Award:	Newbery Honor Book

Kid, 12 years old

Written by HJK16 Excellent read!

Read about Minli's adventure and the people she meets. She runs away from home. Gives you a glimpse of Chinese culture.

Kid, 11 years old

Written by Ollie30 Awesome read!

Awesome story. Very different from anything that I have read before. It is a narrative story, but also includes myths and legends. I love myths and legends – five stars!

Transfer of skills: Do you know where China is located? Can you find it on a map? Can you say the word 'China' in other languages? Let's take a look.

An tSín (Irish), *Kinija* (Lithuanian), *Cina* (Italian), *Hiina* (Estonian)

> **My reading goal** ★ Read for deeper meaning.

Where the Mountain Meets the Moon

Chapter 3

But the goldfish was real, and when her parents returned from the fields for dinner they were not happy to learn that Minli had spent her money on it.

'How could you spend your money on that!' Ma said, <u>slapping the rice bowls</u> on the table. 'On something so useless? And we will have to feed it! There is barely enough rice for us as it is.'

'I will share my rice with it,' Minli said quickly. 'The goldfish man said that it will <u>bring fortune to our house</u>.'

'Fortune!' Ma said. 'You spend half the money in our house!'

'Now, Wife,' Ba said, sitting quietly, 'it was Minli's money. It was hers to do with as she wished. Money must be used sometime. What use is money in a bowl?'

'It is more useful than a goldfish in a bowl,' her mother said shortly.

'Who knows,' Ba said. 'Maybe it will bring fortune to our house.'

'Another <u>impossible dream</u>,' Ma said, looking at the plain rice in her bowl with bitterness. 'It will take more than a goldfish to bring fortune to our house.'

'Like what?' Minli asked. 'What do we need to bring fortune here?'

'Ah,' Ba said, 'that is a question you will have to ask the Old Man of the Moon.'

'The Old Man of the Moon again,' Minli said, and she looked at her father. 'Ba, you said you would tell me the Old Man of the Moon story again today.'

'More stories!' Ma said, and her chopsticks struck the inside of her empty rice bowl resentfully. 'Haven't we had enough of those?'

'Now, Wife,' Ba said again, 'stories cost us nothing.'

'And gain us nothing as well,' Ma said.

There was <u>a stony silence</u> as Ba looked sadly into his rice bowl. Minli tugged at his sleeve. 'Please, Ba?' she said.

Ma shook her head and sighed, but said nothing and Ba began.

50

The Story of the Old Man of the Moon

Once there was a **magistrate** who was quite powerful and proud. He was so proud that he demanded constant respect from his people. Whenever he made a trip out of the city, no matter what time of day or night, people were to leave their homes, get on their knees, and make deep bows as he passed, or else face the brutal punishment of his soldiers. The magistrate was fierce in his anger as well as his pride. It is said he even expected the monkeys to come down from the trees to bow to him.

The magistrate was harsh with his **subordinates**, ruthless to his enemies and pitiless to his people. All feared his wrath and when he roared his orders the people trembled. Behind his back, they called him Magistrate Tiger.

Magistrate Tiger's most **coveted** wish was to be of royal blood. His every decision was crafted for that purpose; every **manipulation** was part of a strategy to achieve acceptance into the **imperial** family. As soon as his son was born, he began to make trips and inquiries to gain influence, in hopes that he could marry his son to a member of the imperial family.

One night, as the magistrate travelled through the mountains (again on a trip to gain favour for his son's future marriage), he saw an old man sitting alone in the moonlight. The old man ignored the passing horses and carriages, the silk brocade and the government seal, and simply continued reading a large book in his lap, placidly fingering a bag of red string beside him. The old man's indifference **infuriated** Magistrate Tiger and he ordered the carriage to stop. However, even the halting noises did not make the old man look up.

Finally, Magistrate Tiger exited his carriage and walked up to the old man, who was still **engrossed** in his book.

'Do you not bow to your magistrate?' he roared.

The old man continued to read.

'What are you reading that is so important?' the magistrate demanded, and looked at the pages of the book. It was full of scribbles and scrawls that weren't of any language the magistrate knew of. 'Why, it is just nonsense written in there!'

'Nonsense!' the old man said, finally looking up. 'You fool. This is the Book of Fortune. It holds all the knowledge of the world – the past, the present and the future.'

The magistrate looked again at the marks on the page. 'I cannot read it,' he said.

'Of course not,' the man said. 'But I, the Old Man of the Moon, Guardian of the Book of Fortune, can read it. And with it, I can answer any question in the world.'

'You can answer any question in the world?' the magistrate **scoffed**. 'Very well. Who will my son marry when he is of age?'

The Old Man of the Moon flipped the pages of the book. 'Hmmm,' he said to himself. 'Yes, here it is … your son's future wife is now the two-year-old daughter of a grocer in the next village.'

'The daughter of a grocer!' the magistrate spat.

'Yes,' the Old Man of the Moon continued. 'Right now she is wrapped in a blue blanket embroidered with white rabbits, sitting on the lap of her blind grandmother in front of her house.'

'No!' the magistrate said. 'I won't allow it!'

'It's true,' the Old Man said. 'They are destined to be husband and wife. I, myself, tied the red cord that binds them.'

'What red cord?' Magistrate Tiger demanded.

'Do you know nothing? I tie together everyone who meets with these red threads.' The Old Man sighed, holding up his bag full of red string. 'When you were born, I tied your ankle to your wife's ankle with a red thread, and as you both grew older the line became shorter until you eventually met. All the people you've met in your life have been brought to you by the red cords I tied. I must have forgotten to tie the end of one of the lines, which is why you are meeting me now. I won't do that again.'

'I don't believe you,' the magistrate said.

'Believe or don't believe,' the Old Man said, standing up and putting the big book on his back. 'We have reached the end of our thread and I will now leave.'

The magistrate stared in <u>dumbfounded silence</u> as the Old Man of the Moon walked up the mountain.

'Crazy old man,' the magistrate said finally. 'What a waste of my time!'

The magistrate returned to his carriage and continued on. But as they drove through the next village he saw an old blind woman holding a baby girl in front of a house. The girl was wrapped in a blue blanket embroidered with white rabbits, just as the Old Man of the Moon had said.

Magistrate Tiger burned with anger. 'I will not let my son marry a grocer's daughter!' he vowed. So, after he arrived at his guesthouse, the magistrate secretly ordered one of his servants to return to the grocer's home and stab the girl with a knife. That will take care of her, he thought to himself.

Many years later, Magistrate Tiger had his dream fulfilled. He was finally able to obtain a match for his son with one of the emperor's many granddaughters, and his son would **inherit** the rule of a remote city.

On the wedding day, Magistrate Tiger bragged to his son about how he had arranged the marriage and **outwitted** the Old Man of the Moon. The son (who was not like his father) said nothing, but after the wedding ceremony, sent a trusted servant to find the grocer's family to make **amends**. In the meantime, he became acquainted with his bride and was happy to find that both were pleased with each other. He found his new wife beautiful, the only **oddity** about her being that she always wore a delicate flower on her forehead.

'Dear Wife,' he said, 'why do you always wear that flower? Even to sleep, you never remove it.'

'It is to hide my scar,' she said, touching her forehead in embarrassment. 'When I was a child no older than two, a strange man stabbed me with a knife. I survived, but I still have this scar.'

And at that moment, the trusted servant came rushing in. 'Master,' he said, 'I made the inquiry you asked for. In a flood many years ago, the grocer's family perished – except for the daughter. The king of the city (the emperor's ninth son) then adopted the daughter and raised her as his own … and that daughter is your wife!'

***

'So the Old Man of the Moon was right!' Minli said.

'Of course he was,' Ba replied. 'The Old Man of the Moon knows everything and can answer any question you ask.'

'I should ask him to bring fortune to our house!' Minli said. 'He would know, I'll ask him. Where do I find him?'

'They say he lives on top of Never-Ending Mountain,' Ba said. 'But no one I have ever spoken to knows where that is.'

'Maybe we can find out,' Minli said.

'Oh, Minli!' Ma said impatiently. 'Bringing fortune to our house! Making Fruitless Mountain bloom! You're always wishing to do impossible things! Stop believing stories and stop wasting your time!'

'Stories are not a waste of time,' Ba said.

Carlos and Isabel's Response

¡Hola de nuevo! (Hello again!) We chose the book for our book talk and we loved it. What do you think? Would you like to read more?

Book Talk: *Where the Mountain Meets the Moon*

Do you like stories about adventure? Do you like stories about other cultures? If you do, this book is for you!

This story is about a young Chinese girl called Minli. She comes from a very poor family who lives in the village at the base of Fruitless Mountain. She loves listening to her father's stories. One day she spends her money on a goldfish. Regretting her decision, she decides to go to the Never-Ending Mountain to change her family's fortune.

Read Grace Lin's book to find out more about the challenges Minli will face on her quest to find the Old Man of the Moon, who possesses the power to change a person's fortune.

What do you think of our book talk? It has to be short. Is there anything we can improve on? We didn't give the ending away – that would ruin it for everyone!

> Who will Minli meet along the way? Will she succeed? Will she not? What lessons will she learn?

Author's Intent

How has this author slightly changed the structure of narrative stories?

What message do you think she is trying to get across?

Dragon Dance
by Max Fatchen

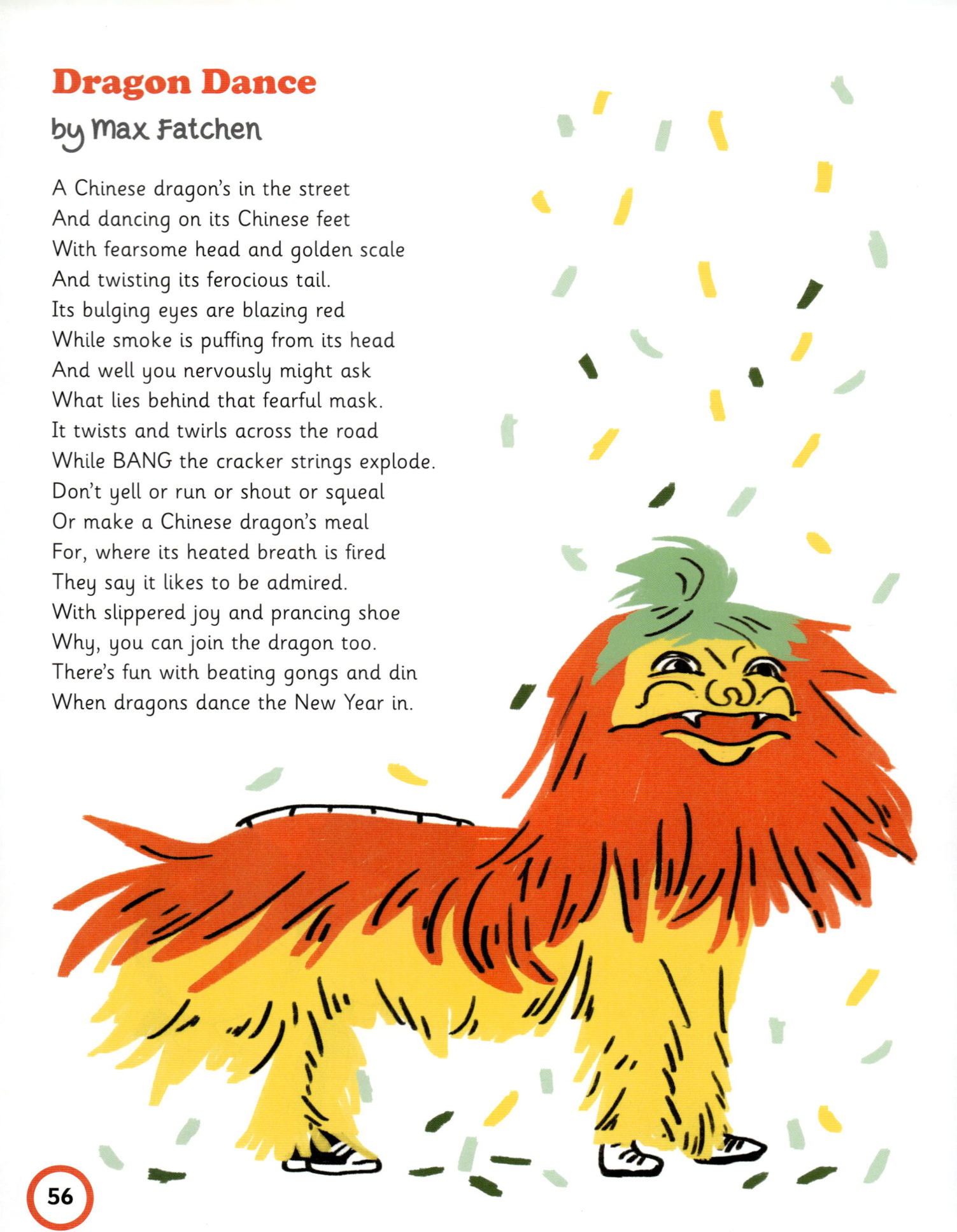

A Chinese dragon's in the street
And dancing on its Chinese feet
With fearsome head and golden scale
And twisting its ferocious tail.
Its bulging eyes are blazing red
While smoke is puffing from its head
And well you nervously might ask
What lies behind that fearful mask.
It twists and twirls across the road
While BANG the cracker strings explode.
Don't yell or run or shout or squeal
Or make a Chinese dragon's meal
For, where its heated breath is fired
They say it likes to be admired.
With slippered joy and prancing shoe
Why, you can join the dragon too.
There's fun with beating gongs and din
When dragons dance the New Year in.

Narrative

Christmas

Blanka's Intro

Wesołych Świąt! (Happy Christmas!) Are you counting down now? How many more days till your holidays? Do you have your Christmas tree up? I can't wait for Christmas Eve. It's tradition on Christmas Eve in my country to eat a big feast. There is usually a selection of 12 dishes! We eat *pierogi*. They are Polish dumplings stuffed with different fillings such as cheese and vegetables. They are scrumptious.

> This week we are going to read a **narrative** script. It's a piece of writing in the form of a drama. It includes characters, setting, plot and a theme. A narrative text consists of paragraphs, while a narrative script consists of dialogue – what the characters say to each other. The dialogue is set out with the character's name on the left, then a colon (:) and then the dialogue. Play scripts are generally written for the stage.

Do you have any special traditions during Christmas? We are going to get into the festive spirit by reading an extract from *A Christmas Carol* by Charles Dickens. Have you heard of it? When you read this script, it's important that you use your vocal expression to help the audience understand the story, as there are no costumes, sets or movement. I'm excited to see what you think!

Transfer of skills: Christmas is celebrated in many countries around the world. Can you say 'Happy Christmas' in other languages? Let's take a look.

Nollaig Shona (Irish), *Feliz Navidad* (Spanish), *Joyeux Noël* (French), *Buon Natale* (Italian)

> **My reading goal** ★ Develop fluency through repeated practice.

A Christmas Carol

Act One: Marley's Ghost

Six roles are needed: Narrator, Nephew (a cheerful young man), Scrooge (a grumpy old man), Gentleman (a kindly man), Marley (a whining ghost) and a Flame (scared).

NARRATOR: Once upon a time, upon a Christmas Eve, old Scrooge sat busy in his **counting-house**.

NEPHEW: A merry Christmas, uncle!

NARRATOR It was the voice of Scrooge's nephew.

SCROOGE: Bah! Humbug!

NEPHEW: Christmas a **humbug**, uncle! You don't mean that, I am sure?

SCROOGE: I do. Out upon merry Christmas! If I had my will, every idiot who goes about with 'Merry Christmas' on his lips should be boiled with his own pudding. He should!

NEPHEW: Uncle!

SCROOGE: Nephew, keep Christmas in your own way, and let me keep it in mine.

NEPHEW: Keep it! But you don't keep it.

SCROOGE: Let me leave it alone, then. Much good may it do you! Much good it has ever done you!

NEPHEW: I have always thought of Christmas time as a good time; a kind, forgiving, charitable, pleasant time. And therefore, uncle, though it has never put a scrap of gold or silver in my pocket, I believe that it has done me good, and will do me good; and I say, God bless it!

SCROOGE: Good afternoon.

NEPHEW: I'll keep my Christmas humour to the last. So a Merry Christmas, uncle!

SCROOGE: GOOD afternoon!

NEPHEW: And a Happy New-Year!

SCROOGE: GOOD AFTERNOON!

NARRATOR: His nephew left the room without an angry word, but the clerk, in letting Scrooge's nephew out, had let one other person in.

GENTLEMAN: At this festive season of the year, Mr Scrooge, we should make some slight provision for the poor and **destitute**, who suffer greatly at the present time. A few of us are **endeavouring** to raise a fund to buy the poor some meat and drink, and means of warmth. What shall I put you down for?

SCROOGE: Nothing!

GENTLEMAN: You wish to be **anonymous**?

SCROOGE: I wish to be left alone. Since you ask me what I wish, that is my answer. I don't make merry myself at Christmas and I can't afford to make **idle** people merry. I help to support the prisons and the **workhouses** – they cost enough – and those who are badly off must go there.

GENTLEMAN: Many can't go there; and many would rather die.

SCROOGE: If they would rather die, they had better do it!

NARRATOR: The hour of shutting up the counting-house arrived. Scrooge took his **melancholy** dinner in his usual melancholy **tavern** and went home to bed. Now it is a fact that there was nothing at all particular about the knocker on the door of this house, except that it was very large; and yet Scrooge, having his key in the lock of the door, saw in the knocker, not a knocker, but Marley's face. Marley's face, with a **dismal** light about it, like a bad lobster in a dark cellar. As Scrooge looked at this, it was a knocker again. He said, 'Pooh, pooh!' … and closed the door with a BANG.

The sound **resounded** through the house like thunder. (BANG, Bang, bang) Every room above, and every cask in the wine-merchant's cellars below (BANG, Bang, bang), appeared to have a separate peal of echoes (BANG, Bang, bang) of its own. Scrooge was not a man to be frightened by echoes. He fastened the door and walked across the hall and up the stairs.

Up Scrooge went, not caring a button for its being very dark. Darkness is cheap and Scrooge liked it.

Quite satisfied, he closed his door and locked himself in; double-locked himself in, which was not his custom. Thus secured against surprise, he put on his dressing-gown and slippers and his nightcap and sat down before the very low fire to take his gruel.

NARRATOR: As he threw his head back in the chair, his glance happened upon a bell, a disused bell, that hung in the room. It was with great astonishment, and with a strange dread, that, as he looked, he saw this bell begin to swing. (*ding, ding, ding*) Soon it rang out loudly (*Ding, DING, DING!*) and so did every bell in the house. (*Dingaling, Aling, ALing, ALING, ALING, ALING, ALING!*)

This was succeeded by a clanking noise (*clank*) deep down below (*clank*), as if some person (*clank*) were dragging a heavy chain (*clank*) over the casks in the wine-merchant's cellar.

Then he heard the noise much louder (*Clank*) on the floors below (*Clank*); then coming up the stairs (*Clank!*); then coming straight towards his door. (*Clank!!*)

It came on through the heavy door (*CLANK!!!*) and a **spectre** passed into the room before his eyes. And upon its coming in, the dying flame leaped up, as though it cried,

FLAME: I know him! Marley's ghost!

SCROOGE: What do you want with me?

MARLEY: Much!

SCROOGE: Who are you?

MARLEY: Ask me who I was.

SCROOGE: Who were you, then?

MARLEY: In life I was your partner, Jacob Marley.

NARRATOR: The ghost sat down on the opposite side of the fireplace, as if he were quite used to it.

MARLEY: You don't believe in me.

SCROOGE: I don't.

MARLEY: Why do you doubt your senses?

SCROOGE: Because a little thing affects them. You may be an undigested bit of beef, a blot of mustard, a crumb of cheese, a fragment of an underdone potato. There's more of gravy than of grave about you, whatever you are!

NARRATOR: The spirit raised a frightful cry …

MARLEY: [HOWL] OOOOOOOOHHHHHHHHHHHHHHHH

SCROOGE Mercy! Dreadful **apparition**, why do you trouble me? Why do spirits walk the earth, and why do they come to me?

MARLEY: It is required of every man, that the spirit within him should walk among his fellow-men, and travel far and wide; and if that spirit goes not forth in life, it is **condemned** to do so after death. I cannot rest, I cannot stay, I cannot linger anywhere. My spirit never walked beyond our counting-house – mark me! – in life my spirit never roved beyond our money-changing hole; and weary journeys lie before me!

NARRATOR: Scrooge was very much dismayed to hear the spectre going on at this rate, and began to quake exceedingly.

MARLEY: I am here tonight to warn you that you have yet a chance and hope of escaping my fate. You will be haunted by Three Spirits. Expect the first tomorrow night, when the bell tolls one. Expect the second on the next night at the same hour. The third, upon the next night, when the last stroke of twelve has ceased to vibrate. Look to see me no more.

Blanka's Response

What do you think of my poem?

Christmas Eve Scrooge sat in his counting-house,
Humbug, humbug, humbug,
Rude to his nephew,
Inconsiderate to the poor,
Sat on his own,
To his dismay the bell rang aloud.
Marley the ghost appeared
And warned him of his fate,
So he will be haunted by three ghosts!

I hope you enjoyed the script! Actors and actresses use scripts for films. They learn their scripts off by heart. Did you ever have to learn a script off by heart? Was it hard or easy?

Jim Carrey played Scrooge in the movie version of *A Christmas Carol*. I wonder what techniques he uses to learn a script off by heart? *A Christmas Carol* is one of my favourite movies to watch over Christmas. What films will you be watching over Christmas?

Author's Intent

What do you think best describes the main reason the author wrote this: to provide readers with information, to describe a person, event or issue? To persuade readers to think about an issue in a certain way and to take action? Or to entertain?

Dave Dirt's Christmas Presents
by Kit Wright

Dave Dirt wrapped his Christmas presents
Late on Christmas Eve
And gave his near relations things
That you would not believe.

His brother got an Odour-Eater –
Second-hand one, natch.
For Dad he chose, inside its box,
A single burnt-out match.

His sister copped the sweepings from
His hairy bedroom rug,
While Mum received a centipede
And Granny got a slug.

Next day he had the nerve to sit
Beneath the Christmas tree
And say: 'OK, I've done my bit –
What have you got for me?'

Persuasive Writing

Gaming

Blanka's Intro

Cześć! (Hey!) How is everyone? My *Over the Moon* friends have come along for this unit to share their opinions on gaming. Do you like gaming? I love it!

Today, millions of players compete in 'massively multiplayer online role-playing games' (MMORPGs), many spending long hours battling with friends online. There are endless ways to play, from mobile apps to virtual-reality headsets, from the moment we wake up to last thing at night. And in a world of likes, shares and followers, our whole lives can feel like a game. Now try to imagine a world without games or player rankings. How would this make you feel?

> This week we are looking at **persuasive writing**. Persuasive writing shares a particular point of view or opinion. The goal of persuasive writing is to persuade the reader by arguing one side of the topic.
>
> Look out for persuasive writing features:
>
> - **Title:** This implies a point of view.
> - **Introduction:** This gives the reader an idea of what the writing is about.
> - **Paragraphs:** The paragraphs are arguments presented to the reader. The author gives reasons to entice the reader to change their mind or do something.
> - **Conclusion:** The author's point of view is repeated.

My friends and I have all been arguing about whether or not gaming is good or bad for you. What do you think? Take a class poll. We have been divided into two teams:

- **Team 1:** Alex and Isabel – Gaming is good for you
- **Team 2:** Tom and Ella – Gaming is bad for you

Have a read of our persuasive writing. Which team are you backing?

> **Transfer of skills:** Gaming is a very popular pastime. Can you say the words 'computer gaming' in other languages? What do you notice?
>
> *ríomhchluichíocht* (Irish), *gry komputerowe* (Polish), *juegos de computadora* (Spanish), *jeux informatiques* (French)

My reading goal ★ Pay close attention to the tone of the author (for example, is it serious, dismissive, formal, optimistic?), as the tone can be used to influence or persuade the reader.

Gaming

Alex: Gaming Is Good for You

I strongly believe that gaming is good for you. My reason for this belief is that playing video games has health benefits for both the brain and the body. It enables us to exercise our brains and bodies in numerous ways.

To begin with, video games can help you to keep fit, which is **necessary** for overall good health. Games such as Wii Sports and Wii Fit are beneficial exercise games, or 'exergames'. They are games that require players to apply physical movements to **manipulate** the actions of the characters in the video game. They include sports such as baseball, bowling, boxing, golf and tennis. Research has shown that playing these games increases heart rate and oxygen intake, which translates to calories being burned. Exergames get players up and moving, helping with **circulation**, joint flexibility, co-ordination and balance. Many of these same games track your progress and even help you to set goals to keep you motivated.

In addition, playing action video games benefits hand–eye co-ordination. Action games require the players to react quickly and accurately to events that happen on the screen. There are many professions that require better than average hand–eye co-ordination, such as machine operators, airline pilots and surgeons. Surgeons depend on hand–eye co-ordination to perform successful operations.

Many aspiring surgeons are now required to perform virtual surgeries for training. Scientists at the University of Texas Medical Branch brought together a group of secondary school kids, college students and medical residents to perform these virtual surgeries. After testing the three groups to see who could **outperform** the others, the scientists discovered that the secondary school students did the best. This was due to the time spent by secondary school students playing video games.

My final reason for arguing that gaming is good for you is due to the fact that it improves memory, focus and attention. A study carried out at the University of California found that a group of students improved their memory by 12% after two weeks playing Super Mario 3D World. This demonstrates that video games can help to improve our memory, in particular, 3D games that require problem-solving in order to progress and complete **objectives**. Playing video games requires high levels of attention. It exercises many of the **cognitive** skills that help you to pay attention and stay on task. It requires you to make fast-paced decisions and identify relevant and important details.

To conclude, I believe that gaming is good for you. Every child should be allowed to game, as it helps you to stay fit, improves hand–eye co-ordination and memory and helps you to focus. Gaming can be a powerful tool in improving mental and physical health.

> Impressive! Alex definitely did his homework. He has supported his points with research. What do you think? Are you persuaded that gaming is good for you? Will Alex's team win? Let's read on to see what Tom's persuasive speech is.

Tom: The Negative Effects of Gaming

I strongly believe that gaming is bad for you. I personally believe that playing video games can have a negative impact on your physical and mental health. I have several reasons for arguing for this point of view.

My first reason is that playing video games requires you to sit in one position. According to the most recent research, sitting down puts your body on standby. When you do it for long enough, your **metabolism** slows down. Therefore, you are not burning any calories. This can lead to health problems such as **obesity** and high cholesterol levels.

While playing 'exergames' such as Wii Sports is an option, they do not produce as good a fitness benefit as playing the real sport. The energy a person spends playing video games could be better spent elsewhere, such as playing football, swimming, going for a walk, cycling or skateboarding. As Cedric X. Bryant, chief science officer of a non-profit exercise organisation, points out, while 'Wii Sports offer more of a cardio benefit than sedentary games, we believe there is no substitute for the real sport'.

Another reason I believe gaming is bad for your health is due to the fact that gaming is very addictive. Video games are intentionally designed using state-of-the-art behaviour psychology to keep you hooked. Games are so immersive that it's easy to play for hours and hours without even noticing that a minute has gone by. Before you know it, you have spent a lot of time by yourself. This time could be better spent with family and friends. Furthermore, it has been claimed that excessive time spent on gaming has led to poor diet choices and sleep deprivation. It is important to understand and know that video game addiction exists because game companies are billion-dollar industries and the more people they have hooked on games, the more money they make. The World Health Organization recognises video game addiction as 'gaming disorder'.

In addition, as mentioned briefly above, excessive amounts of time spent on gaming can have negative effects on your social interactions. Gaming is an indoor activity. Gamers sit in isolated areas of the house to play video games. For example, they play gaming in their bedrooms, so there is less opportunity for social interaction. This can impact the quality of relationships with parents, siblings and friends.

Without a doubt, it is clear to see the negative impacts of gaming. Gaming does not help you to stay fit, it can be addictive and it can cause poor relationships with families and friends. Overall, time would be better spent connecting with family or friends through activities such as hillwalking, mountain climbing, sightseeing and making the most of what the outdoors has to offer.

Wow! Some fantastic points by Tom. Do you see how he counterargued Alex's point on Wii Sports? Do you think he made some valid points? Have you switched over to Tom's team? We are now going to hear from Isabel and Ella.

Isabel: Gaming Has Many Benefits

In my opinion, gaming is good for you.

When you're in the middle of a game, does the time stand still? Concentrating hard allows us to forget our everyday worries, whether it's skipping stones across a lake, building teetering towers out of wooden blocks or filling out a crossword puzzle on the train. In video games, you can go a step further by entering a fantasy world filled with bizarre challenges and fantastical creatures. You can create your own avatar and follow your friends and family on the other side of the world.

It seems that most people think gaming is anti-social, but this could not be further from the truth. Gaming can be very social. Playing video games gives you the opportunity to make friends, chat or work in a team. There are video games that have the option of online gaming. With this option, a person has the opportunity to socialise with other people worldwide who are also playing video games. A lot of **interaction** is going on when gaming online.

To conclude, gaming is fun, there is a game to suit everybody's interests and it's a great way for the family to get together and play.

Ella: Gaming Causes Problems

I *strongly* believe that gaming is bad for you.

Gaming can be obsessive. Games often include lots of levels, which can often mean that you become fixated on completing levels. Often gamers will not stop playing because they are close to reaching the next level and continue to play. As a result, too much times is spent playing video games.

The most popular types of games nowadays are violent games. There are virtual reality games that encourage violent behaviour. It becomes heroic to do evil things. Players are encouraged to fight, use guns, set off bombs, etc. These games do not encourage good moral values.

In conclusion, gaming is bad for you. I believe too much time can be spent on gaming and that video games can negatively shape our morals.

Blanka's Response

> These are some brilliant persuasive texts. What did you think? Which team is the winning team? Alex and Isabel or Tom and Ella?

It seems to me that both teams put forward some excellent points. However, I personally believe 'everything in moderation'. Too much of anything is never good for you, and it's hard to get enough exercise if you're always watching a screen. It's true that certain video games can improve your co-ordination, while your ability to work out the trickiest levels gives you confidence to solve even the most difficult problems. But too much gaming can lead to health issues. Always remember that the best games are the right ones for your age.

Keep these tips in mind when you're gaming!

Gaming Top Tips

Five signs you're gaming too much:

- When you stop playing, you get upset or bored.
- You spend less time hanging out with friends.
- It's hard to concentrate at school.
- You lie about how often and for how long you're gaming.
- You feel guilty about this, but you can't stop.

Author's Intent

Why do you think the author wrote this extract?

Did the author influence your response (views or opinions) towards this particular topic?

Computer Boot

by Kenn Nesbitt

When I powered my computer on today
it wouldn't boot,
so I tapped it just a little
but it still would not compute.

So I thumped a little harder
hoping that would make it go.
When it didn't help, I hit it with
an even bigger blow.

Then I punched it half a dozen times
which wasn't very smart,
for my knuckles hurt like heck
but my computer didn't start.

So I whacked it with a hammer
and I knocked it over flat,
and I probably should not have clubbed it
with my baseball bat.

But at least I didn't fret about
it booting anymore,
since I booted my computer
down the stairs and out the door.

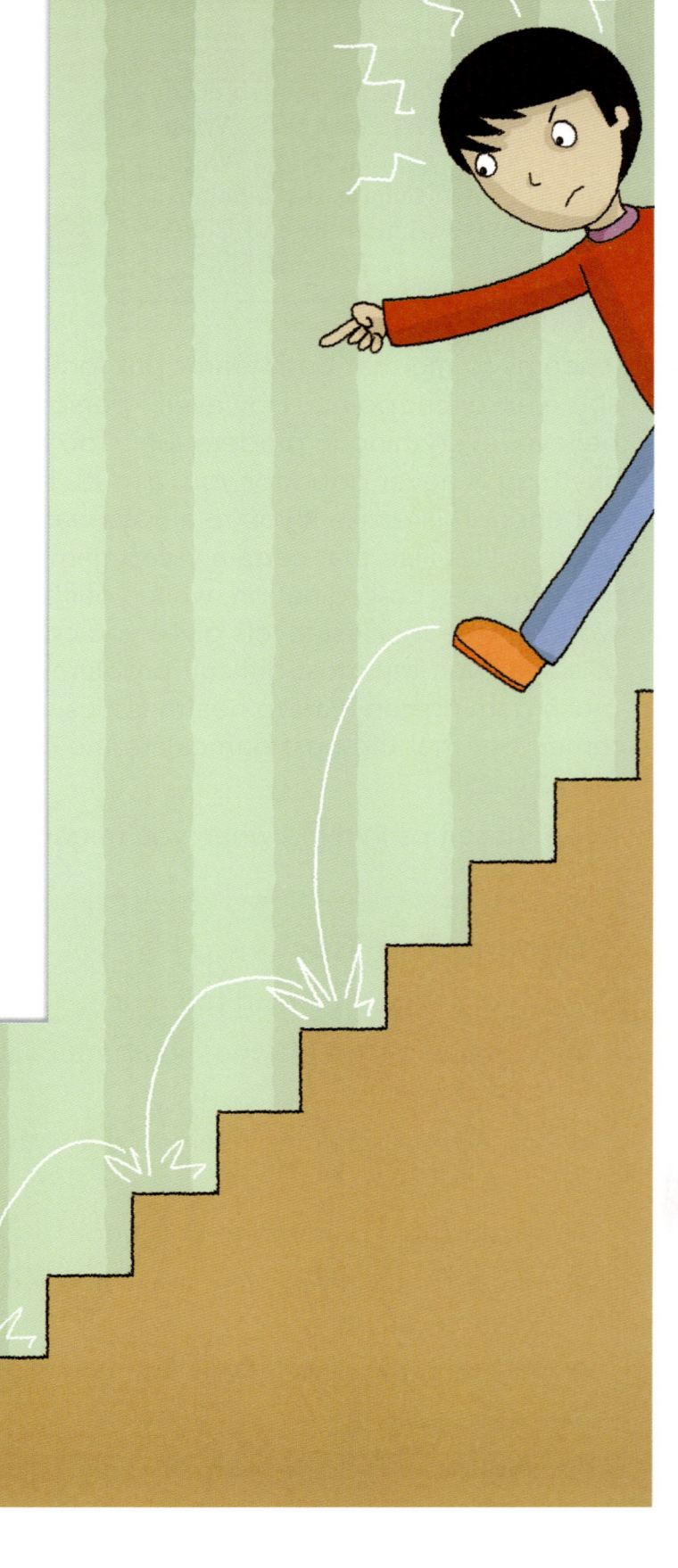

Persuasive Writing

World War One

Tom's Intro

Dia daoibh, a chairde. This week we are going to go to back in time to the year 1914. World War One began on 28 July 1914 and it lasted until 11 November 1918. This extract is going to give you many reasons why you wouldn't want to be in the trenches in World War One!

This extract is an example of **persuasive writing**. The purpose of persuasive texts is to convince you to change your mind about a topic or to do something. Examples of persuasive texts can include advertisements, such as a travel brochure enticing you to visit the World War One battlefields or a poster enticing you to buy the Battleship game.

Persuasive writing includes the following features:

- **Title:** This implies a point of view.
- **Introduction:** This gives the reader an idea of what the writing is about.
- **Paragraphs:** The paragraphs are arguments presented to the reader. The author gives reasons to entice the reader to change their mind or do something.
- **Conclusion:** The author's point of view is repeated.
- **Language:** Powerful adjectives and verbs are used.

I chose this text by Alex Woolf because I love history. It is one of my favourite subjects. I also love playing war games. Battleship is one my favourite games. I'm really eager to find out all the reasons why you wouldn't want to be in the trenches in World War One. My mind is racing and I can already think of a few reasons – can you?

Transfer of skills: Do you know what 'world war' is in another language? What do you notice?

cogadh domhanda (Irish), *weltkrieg* (German), *guerra mondiale* (Italian), *guerra mundial* (Portuguese)

> **My reading goal** ★ Visualise to understand and learn what it was like to be in the trenches.

You Wouldn't Want to Be in the Trenches in World War One!

Introduction

It's August 1914. You are Tommy Atkins, living in London. War has just broken out in Europe. The Allies, led by Britain, France and Russia, are fighting the Central Powers, led by Germany. You're very proud of your country. Britain is the most powerful nation in the world, with an enormous global empire. But recently, Germany's grown powerful too, and now is challenging Britain for the role of top superpower. In Britain everyone is very enthusiastic about the war and confident of victory. You get swept up in the excitement. Many people **optimistically** predict a victory by Christmas. Little do they know that because of new weapons and **tactics** the conflict will drag on for four years and will be one of the bloodiest, most gruesome wars ever fought.

Training

You are sent to your regimental depot where you receive your kit, then to a training camp to join your **battalion**. Here you get your first taste of army discipline and training. You sleep in a tent because there aren't enough huts. There are shortages of kit and equipment, and for the first few days you train in your own shoes and a red jacket dating back to the Boer War from 1899 to 1902. There's also a shortage of officers because all the experienced ones are in France, fighting. Men have been brought out of retirement to train recruits. One gives out instructions while sitting in a chair.

New Skills

You're given training in physical fitness, how to march, first aid and how to defend yourself against a gas attack. You're also taught basic field skills, like how to handle your weapons safely, fire a gun, throw a **grenade** and fight with a bayonet.

To France

After just a few weeks' training, you're sent to a camp in northern France. You see the wounded returning from the front.

> Right, I've taken this pin thing out, now what do I do?

The Trenches

You go 'up the line' to the trenches. The **trench** at the front is the 'fire trench' and behind that are rows of support and reserve trenches where you can fall back if under attack. Beyond the fire trench is 'no-man's-land', then the German trenches. These lines of opposing trenches stretch all the way from the North Sea to Switzerland. You quickly learn that life in the trenches can be both tough and boring. Every day begins with a 'stand-to' an hour before dawn, when the enemy is most likely to attack; every man has to stand on the fire step for an hour or more, rifle loaded, bayonet fixed.

Boring Days

When not on sentry duty or digging, soldiers retire to their dug-outs. They fill their idle moments writing letters, playing cards or singing songs.

Busy Nights

Trenches are often busiest at night, when soldiers can't be spotted by the enemy. Trenches are repaired and teams sent out into no-man's-land to collect the dead and wounded.

I want my breakfast.

I want my bed.

Be quiet or we're taking you back.

Rats and Lice

You are forced to share your trench with some quite unpleasant creatures, including frogs, horned beetles and fat red slugs. Worst of all are the rats and lice.

Rats Get Fat

The rats eat your **rations** and spread disease among your comrades. Some grow as large as cats by eating unburied corpses. They show no fear of you and crawl all over you while you sleep.

Rat-a-Tat-Tat

Soldiers fight back by shooting rats. If the sergeant catches them, they'll be put on a charge for wasting ammo. Sometimes men bait the ends of their rifles with bacon to get a shot at close quarters.

Hands up, you dirty rat!

Of Lice and Men

Lice are another annoying trench pest. They itch like crazy, leave red blotches on the victim's body and spread diseases such as trench fever and **typhus**.

Chatting

Lice hunting is called 'chatting'. Soldiers kill lice by running a thumbnail – or sometimes a lit candle – up the seams of their shirt and trousers, where the lice are most deeply **entrenched**.

Bully Beef, Bread and Biscuits

Your daily ration of food is pretty awful. It's mainly bully beef (canned corned beef), maconochie (a stew of meat, turnips and carrots) and bread. You may also eat biscuits and jam. The jam is almost always plum and apple.

Making Do

By 1916, flour is in such short supply that bread is made from ground turnips, sometimes with added sawdust. Meat may be horse or dog. 'Vegetable' soups and stews are made with weeds and nettles picked from nearby fields.

Foul Flavours

The British kitchen staff prepare all the food in the same large vats. As a result, everything tastes of something else.

Yum, tea-flavoured soup!

Hard Biscuits

It takes up to eight days for bread to reach the front line, so it's always stale. The biscuits are so hard, soldiers often soak them in water for a few days, then heat and drain them and add some condensed milk. The resulting mush is said to be quite edible.

Cool Cuisine

By the time food reaches the front line it's always cold. Sometimes a group of soldiers manage to obtain a cooking stove so they can heat their food and brew some tea.

The Cold and the Wet

Autumn turns to winter with no sign of an end to the war. There is constant rain. Trenches become rivers and frequently collapse. The rains have caused the latrines to overflow into the trenches, spreading disease. Some soldiers prefer to risk death by sleeping outside the trenches. When on sentry duty, you're forced to stand in a freezing, waterlogged trench for hours on end without being able to remove your wet socks or boots. Your feet have gone numb and the skin is turning blue. You have trench foot! Luckily for you, it's treated before it goes **gangrenous**. Otherwise it might have had to be amputated.

Is that you, Briggs?

Under Fire

About 10 million tonnes of artillery shells are fired against enemy positions during World War One. Shelling is constant, reaching its greatest intensity before an attack. After several weeks at the front, the never-ending *boom-boom-boom* is starting to fray your nerves.

You feel tired and **irritable** and get frequent headaches. One of your comrades becomes so distressed that he deliberately wounds himself so that he can go to hospital.

Over the Top!

It is now June 1917. Your squadron is to be part of a major British Army offensive at Messines. An offensive is a large-scale attack on enemy lines using at least a corps (up to 45,000 soldiers). You are excited, nervous and very scared. The battle starts at 4:30 a.m. with an enormous bang. The earth shakes as 600 tonnes of explosive previously laid by miners are detonated under German lines, opening up enormous craters. You wait nervously on the fire step. The whistle blows and you go over the top.

Wounded

During the assault, you get shot. You dive into a shell hole and use your field dressing to treat your wound.

Stretcher Bearers

With just four stretcher bearers per company, you must wait several hours before you are rescued.

Casualty Clearing Station

After your wound has been cleaned, surgery is carried out to remove the bullet.

Back to Blighty

You are sent back to England with other soldiers wounded in battle. You travel by ship across the Channel, then by train to London, where an ambulance picks you up and delivers you to the military hospital. Children run along beside the ambulance cheering. You feel like a returning hero.

Conclusion

Undoubtedly, you wouldn't want to be in the trenches in World War One. For all the reasons above, we can safely draw the conclusion that Tommy endured very tough, dangerous situations. He was lucky to have been sent back to England and to have survived the trenches.

TOM'S RESPONSE

Blimey! That was an eye-opener. There are many reasons why I wouldn't want to be in the trenches in World War One. There were constant shortages, the food sounds horrific, rats and lice spread diseases, rain caused havoc and the constant headaches! This has given me great perspective. I'm thinking how lucky I am. For four years, soldiers had to endure great hardships and threatening situations. Millions of people lost their lives. I definitely wouldn't have liked to have been in their shoes.

I can connect this to the news. In marking the centenary anniversary of the end of World War One, hundreds of people in Co. Sligo lined up to walk in memory of those who lost their lives. It is estimated that 5,000 Sligo men fought in the war.

Are you persuaded? I am. I think the author has definitely used persuasive features. The title clearly implies a point of view. There is an introduction followed by valid reasons and a conclusion.

> What fact persuaded you the most? I must remember to use these features the next time I need Mum or Dad to give me something!

Author's Intent

Do you think the author chose a good title for their story? Why do you think that?

Was the author trying to persuade, inform or entertain the reader?

In Flanders Fields

by John McCrae

In Flanders fields the poppies blow
Between the crosses, row on row,
That mark our place; and in the sky
The larks, still bravely singing, fly
Scarce heard amid the guns below.

We are the Dead. Short days ago
We lived, felt dawn, saw sunset glow,
Loved and were loved, and now we lie
In Flanders fields.

Take up our quarrel with the foe:
To you from failing hands we throw
The torch; be yours to hold it high.
If ye break faith with us who die
We shall not sleep, though poppies grow
in Flanders fields.

Explanation

Space

Alex's Intro

Hi, everyone! This week we are exploring space. What do you know about space?

Did you know that not that long ago, when people looked up at the sky, they thought they were seeing all of space? The stars we see in the night sky are part of the Milky Way galaxy. That's the galaxy we belong to. Edwin Hubble was an American astronomer. He was the first person to discover that there is a whole universe of galaxies beyond the Milky Way, each one filled with stars and planets and lots of other things too. Some galaxies are smaller than our Milky Way and others are larger. With that one discovery, our idea of space exploded. Space was a whole lot bigger than anyone had ever imagined!

> To explain space clearly for you, I have chosen for you to read it through the genre of **explanation**. An explanation text is a non-fiction text. It provides us with information. These texts are written in the present tense and include technical vocabulary.

In this extract from *Space Explained* by *Primary Planet* magazine there will be clear, simple key points to help you understand why Earth is the only habitable planet in our solar system. Are you ready to learn all about space?

Transfer of skills: Space is the zone above and around our planet, where there is no oxygen to breathe. Do you know what the word 'space' is in another language? Let's take a look.

spás (Irish), *przestrzen* (Polish), *plads* (Danish), *tila* (Finnish)

My reading goal ★ Read for information.

Space Explained

What do you know about the planets in our solar system? Do you know how many there are or how close they are to the sun? Is there life on Mars? Are we the only planet with a moon? Is Pluto considered a planet? Well, worry not – we're going on a planetary tour to give you all the information you need to know.

Where Is Planet Earth?

Earth can be found in the solar system. It is one of eight planets that **orbit** the sun. The sun rests in the centre of our solar system and is a yellow dwarf star. Although it appears yellow through Earth's atmosphere, it is actually white in colour!

What Are the Other Planets?

There are eight planets in our solar system, not nine: Mercury, Venus, Earth, Mars, Jupiter, Saturn, Uranus and Neptune. For many years, Pluto was also termed a planet (the furthest one away). But in 2006 this was changed and Pluto became known as a dwarf planet.

What Is Mercury Like?

The closest planet to the sun, Mercury is roughly one-third of the size of Earth. This planet is very hot, with a daytime temperature of more than 400°C. However, at night, the temperature drops to around −180°C, as there is no atmosphere to keep the heat in. The surface of Mercury is like the surface of our moon – **barren** and rocky, and covered with **craters**. With no atmosphere, there's no wind or any kind of weather and there is no water or air on the surface, although the possibility of water and air existing below the surface has not been ruled out.

What Is Venus Like?

Sometimes called the Morning or Evening Star, Venus (named after the Roman goddess of love) is **visible** from planet Earth and can usually be seen at dusk or sunrise. It has a **molten core** of iron and metal, just like Earth, and is home to more than 100,000 volcanoes. The largest of these is over five miles high – almost the size of Mount Everest! On Venus, the sun rises in the west and sets in the east, as Venus **rotates** in the opposite direction to the Earth. One day on Venus lasts 117 Earth-days!

What Is Earth Like?

Earth is the only planet not named after a god and is the fifth largest planet in our solar system. Under the Earth's crust are plates (called tectonic plates) that move against each other very slowly. This movement results in mountains, hills, volcanoes and earthquakes forming over millions of years. The Earth's **atmosphere**, which acts like a blanket of gases wrapped around the planet, is made up of nitrogen and oxygen. This atmosphere protects us from meteors – which usually burn up before they reach the Earth's surface – and from the heat of the sun.

What Is Mars Like?

Called the Red Planet, Mars has a substance called iron oxide on its surface. It is the fourth planet from the sun and is similar to Earth – it has north and south polar ice caps and its days are only 40 minutes longer than Earth days. Mars also has seasons like Earth, but its temperatures aren't so pleasant – the average summer weather is −5°C. Along with two moons, Phobos and Deimos, Mars is also home to the largest mountain in the entire solar system, Olympus Mons. This stands 25 km in height – three times higher than Everest!

What Is Jupiter Like?

Jupiter is enormous – the biggest of all the planets. In fact, it's so big you could fit 1,300 Earths inside it! Surrounded by thick, colourful clouds of deadly poisonous gases and home to raging gas storms – the biggest of these is known as the Big Red Spot – Jupiter is not a **habitable** planet. It also contains the largest hurricane in our solar system, which has lasted over 300 years to date! The colourful bands seen around Jupiter are caused by the planet whipping up the atmosphere as it spins very quickly.

What Is Saturn Like?

The spectacular rings around Saturn make it a beautiful planet to look at but, like Jupiter, Saturn is a very stormy planet, with winds of up to 800 km/h racing through its atmosphere. The rings around Saturn are made up of millions of ice crystals, some of them as big as a house, with others as tiny as a speck of dust, stretching out into space for thousands of kilometres. It's the second largest planet in the solar system but, as it's mostly made of gas, it's very light. Saturn also has lots of moons orbiting it.

What Is Uranus Like?

The first planet to be discovered by **telescope**, Uranus spins on its side like a barrel – it is thought this may be due to a **collision** early on in its formation. Because it takes 84 Earth-years for Uranus to orbit the sun, this means that each of its poles is in daylight for 42 years and then in darkness for the next 42. Uranus has a blue-green haze caused by high levels of methane gas. Uranus was originally called Georgium Sidus (George's Star) in honour of England's King George III.

What Is Neptune Like?

This planet is made of gas and ice and, as well as being the furthest planet from the sun, it is also the coldest – temperatures can drop to as low as −221°C – cold enough for a human to flash-freeze in a second! Neptune is named after the Roman god of the sea because of its blue ocean-like colour and has 14 moons orbiting it, the largest of which is called Triton. All of Neptune's moons are named after water gods. It takes Neptune 165 Earth-years to orbit the sun, travelling a distance of 4.5 billion kilometres!

How Many Solar Systems Are in the Universe?

One. Our solar system is the ONLY solar system. Everything else is a stellar system or star system. Sol is the name of our sun, hence the name solar system. Our solar system is made up of the sun and the planets. It also includes dwarf planets, moons, asteroids, comets and meteoroids.

What Is a Meteoroid?

A meteoroid is a type of small space rock found in the solar system. They can range from being one metre in width to the size of a grain of rice. Very small meteoroids are called micrometeoroids or space dust.

What Is a Meteor?

A meteor, often called a 'falling star' or a 'shooting star', is the streak of light that comes from space rocks such as meteoroids, comets or asteroids as they pass through Earth's atmosphere.

What Is a Meteorite?

A meteorite is simply the name given to a meteoroid, comet or asteroid when part or all of it makes it to ground. This is not so common, as over 90% of meteoroids, comets or asteroids completely <u>burn up</u> in the atmosphere before reaching the Earth's surface.

What Is an Asteroid?

An asteroid is similar to a meteoroid, except much, much bigger! Although it is much smaller than a planet, it also orbits the sun. Most asteroids can be found in an asteroid belt positioned between Mars and Jupiter and are not considered a danger to Earth. They are sometimes referred to as the oddballs of space <u>due to</u> their irregular shapes and sizes!

Do Asteroids Ever Reach Earth's Surface?

According to NASA (National Aeronautics and Space Administration), about once a year a car-sized asteroid hits Earth's atmosphere. Although this creates an impressive fireball (meteor), it burns up before reaching the surface.

Some asteroids found in the asteroid belt between Mars and Jupiter, and which <u>pose no threat</u> to Earth, can be as big as 900 km in diameter. Ceres is by far the largest asteroid, with a diameter of 975 km!

What Is a Comet?

Often referred to as dirty space snowballs, comets are icy space rocks that release long tails or streaks of gas or dust. Comets can spend millions of years orbiting the sun and can measure between 10 km in size to several hundred. Their tails can be millions of kilometres long! Some comets, such as Halley's Comet, are known as periodic comets. This means they return to the Earth's **vicinity** many times in their lifetime. Halley's Comet appears every 75 years or so. Having last appeared in our skies in 1986, expect a return in mid-2061!

What Is a Galaxy?

A galaxy is a system of millions or billions of stars, together with gas and dust. Our galaxy is known as the Milky Way galaxy. The Milky Way is the galaxy in which we live. It is a spiral-shaped galaxy that contains several hundred billion stars, including our sun.

How Many Galaxies Are There?

The latest scientific studies have discovered that there may well be over 2 trillion galaxies in the universe. Allow us to show you that in numbers: 2,000,000,000,000! And just to remind you, our galaxy alone is made up of billions of stars!

What Is the Universe?

The universe is all of space and time and their contents, including planets, stars, galaxies and all other forms of matter and energy. But get this – many experts in this area **concede** that we only know of one universe because we do not have the technology to see further. Theoretically, there could be billions of other universes, known as 'parallel universes', out there!

Is the Universe Really Expanding?

Yes, it seems so. Scientists can tell this by noting that the galaxies outside of our own are moving away from us, and the ones that are farthest away are moving the fastest.

Will the Universe Ever Cease to Exist?

Yes. But hold on! According to the latest scientific predictions, the universe – now nearly 14 billion years old – should continue to exist for billions of years to come. That's quite a while.

> So, there you have it – space explained in a nutshell. Crikey, I think I need to lie down after all that!

Alex's Response

Wow, so much information. My head is spinning with all those facts!

I think the author did an excellent job of clearly explaining space to us. I really like how the extract is structured. There is a title, subtitles, clear explanations and pictures. What did you think? Did you find it easy to understand?

What facts were you most amazed by? I'm amazed that Jupiter has the largest hurricane in our solar system. I thought Earth was the only planet with hurricanes. I can't believe that temperatures can reach −221°C on Neptune. Imagine flash-freezing in a second – that's a scary thought!

I'm sure you still have lots of questions about space. You should check out NASA's website. They answer some amazing questions, such as:

- Where does the solar system end?
- Why are planets round?
- How long is one day on other planets?

Imagine visiting the Kennedy Space Center in Florida. Wouldn't that be so cool?

Author's Intent

Why do you think the author chose to write about space?
Do you think the author achieved his intended purpose?
Did the extract effectively explain space?

Asteroids
by Elaine Magliaro

A band of old buddies
Sticking together through the years.
Too small to be planets,
Each one a world apart,
Rocky and lifeless,
Orbiting
In unison,
Dancing a ring around the
Sun.

Cinquain Poem

Asteroid
Rocky, Speedy,
Accelerating, Landing, Wrecking,
Asteroids Flying For Planets,
Rock

Asteroids
by Elaine Magliaro

Tiny planets
together in a cosmic kindergarten
holding hands in a circle
playing ring around the sun
yearning to grow up
and have orbits of their own.

Explanation

Volcanoes

Carlos and Isabel's Intro

Carlos
Hola! Cómo estás? I'm really excited to read this unit. It's all about volcanoes.

Isabel
Me too! What genre will we be reading this extract through?

Carlos
It's an **explanation** extract by Elizabeth Rusch. It will explain how volcanoes erupt.

Isabel
Can you remember the features of an explanation text?

Carlos
It has an introduction, a series of steps and a conclusion. It's written in the present tense and uses technical vocabulary.

Isabel
It also has diagrams to help us understand the process.

Carlos
I wonder if any of our friends have ever visited a volcano. We did when we went on holiday to Lanzarote. Lanzarote is known around the world as the 'Island of Volcanoes'. Isabel, can you remember the name of the park we visited?

Isabel
It's called the Timanfaya National Park. It's a shield volcano believed to be 15 million years old. We had such an amazing time. We even got to have a volcanic barbecue!

Carlos
It was awesome. Let's find out about how different volcanoes erupt.

Transfer of skills: There are many volcanoes located around the world. The most active volcanoes are located along the Pacific Rim. It is known as the Ring of Fire. Can you say the word 'volcanoes' in another language? Do you notice any similarities?

bolcán (Irish), *wulkan* (Polish), *volcán* (Spanish), *volcan* (French)

> **My reading goal** ★ Monitor my understanding by paying attention to my reading and use the diagrams/pictures to aid me.

Volcano Rising

KA-BOOM! Most people think volcanoes are either sound asleep or blowing their tops off in fiery, ash-spewing catastrophes. But volcanoes are not just destructive. Much more often, volcanoes are **creative**. They form majestic mountains. And they build new islands where there were none before.

Creative and destructive eruptions start with gooey melted rock called **magma**. Magma from deep in the earth rises up a gigantic straw-like tube to a **vent**, or opening. If magma makes it to the Earth's surface, it's called lava. A burst of **lava** is an eruption.

Magma is made up of gases as well as melted and partially melted rock. As it rises and fills huge underground chambers, pressure builds ... and builds ... and builds ... until the magma is forced up and out a volcano's vent.

Erupted magma can spurt out and flow down a volcano like red-hot syrup. This fluid lava cools to form either spiky chunks called *'a'ā* (ah-aah) or smooth, ropy surfaces called *pāhoehoe* (paah-hoh-eh-hoh-eh).

Magma can also burst out in solid chunks called **tephra** (TEH-frah). Tephra can be tiny bits (ash), lightweight gas-filled pieces (pumice) or solid rocks and boulders (lava bombs). But what determines whether lava erupts peacefully or dangerously?

POW! Gases blast lava out in an explosive eruption.

HISSSSS! Gases and lava slowly seep out in a creative eruption.

Gas determines whether an **eruption** creates or destroys. Rising gas pushes lava out of a volcano. In destructive eruptions, gases get trapped inside thick magma or are blocked by **plugs** in the **vents**. Pressure builds until lava, ash and gases explode all at once, like soda from a shaken can.

In creative eruptions, vents are open and gases escape slowly, like when you carefully unscrew a soda bottle. Lava bubbles and sprays like water from a hose or oozes out like toothpaste from a tube. Layer upon layer of lava piles up, forming lava domes. Over time, peaceful eruptions can build mountains. Creative eruptions occur three times more often than violent ones. They happen all over the world in all kinds of different places.

A creative eruption can start with the ground swelling a tiny bit each year. Magma gathering underground creates a **bulge** that may one day make a new mountain. In the Cascade Range in central Oregon, three composite volcanoes — massive cones made from layers of both lava and ash — sit in a tight cluster, as if they're having a tea party. They're called the Three Sisters: North, Middle and South Sister.

North Sister   *Middle Sister*   *South Sister*

92

Sometimes creation happens more quickly. Volcanoes can appear out of nowhere! One day the ground cracks and ash spurts out, forming a new volcano. In 1943, as a farmer ploughed his cornfield in Paricutín (par-ree-koo-TEEN), Mexico, ash exploded from a crack in the ground, creating a steep cinder cone. In a day the cone reached 50 metres high. In a week it stood 150 metres tall. Ash slowly buried the farm and nearby villages. But the family and villagers moved to land close by and began farming the rich, ash-fertilized fields. After a year Paricutín's cone was more than 330 metres tall. After nine years the <u>cinder-cone volcano</u> stood more than 424 metres. Paricutín is considered one of the wonders of the world. It created a mountain, fertilized fields and gave scientists the chance to study the fast growth of a new volcano.

Paricutín (day one)

Volcanoes even make mountains underwater. If these <u>submarine volcanoes</u> grow high enough, their tips form new islands.

Three-quarters of volcanic activity takes place deep in the ocean. In 1963, a submarine volcano near Iceland erupted to create the island of Surtsey. In a few years the island rose more than 167 metres above sea level and grew to be more than two kilometres across.

Moss and lichen took hold of the lava rocks. A bush grew and then other plants followed. Finally seals, puffins and other animals began breeding there. Surtsey now hosts a small hut for researchers.

Some volcanoes secretly erupt under glaciers, hiding growing mountains deep under thick ice. Grímsvötn (GREEMZ-voe-tihn), Iceland's most frequently active volcano, lies beneath the country's largest glacier. Underneath the vast ice-cap is a hot spot – a place where lots of magma from the Earth's **mantle** rises to the surface. This makes for a very creative volcanic environment, causing Iceland to constantly grow in size.

Surtsey (today)

Most volcanoes have both destructive and creative eruptions. WHAM! They blow their tops. In 1980, Mount St Helens in Washington exploded, shooting a huge black ash cloud higher than airplanes fly and mowing down massive trees as if they were toothpicks.

Even the most dangerous volcanoes – supervolcanoes – can do creative work. Between gigantic eruptions, they can erupt gently for many years, repairing the scarred land. Hundreds of thousands of years ago, the Yellowstone supervolcano had three gigantic eruptions that blanketed most of the United States with ash. So much magma exploded out from underground that the surface collapsed, swallowing mountains and creating a gigantic **crater** called a **caldera**.

Creative volcanoes give us all a chance to witness the power of a volcano rising!

Carlos and Isabel's Response

Carlos
Wow! I never thought of volcanoes being creative.

Isabel
Neither did I! I didn't know that they form new mountains and new islands. What fact did you find the most interesting?

Carlos
I think it is amazing that Iceland continues to grow in size. What did you find intriguing?

Isabel
That three-quarters of volcanic activity takes place in the ocean.

Carlos
What do you think of the extract? I really enjoyed reading it. I think the author did a great job telling us how volcanoes form. She also gave examples of how they can be creative.

Isabel
I agree. What about asking Mamá or Papá if we can visit Iceland? I've already checked flight times, it takes about four hours.

Carlos
Yeah, the flight to Yellowstone might be too long for Mamá, you know she doesn't like flying too much!

Isabel
Let's ask. You know what they say – if you don't ask, you don't get!

Author's Intent

Why do you think the author called this story *Volcano Rising*? Do you think it is a good choice? Why do you think that?

Why do you think she wrote about volcanoes?

Volcano

Magma,
Melted, molten rock,
Like soup that boils in a crock …
Beneath the Earth,
It rolls and roils,
Beneath the Earth,
It turns and toils …
Pressure grows,
Magma escapes,
Blows through holes of different shapes …
Mountain cones,
Ring of Fire,
Volcanoes blow,
Ash flies higher!
Magma flows,
Becomes hot lava,
Cools to make
A place like Java …
Magma comes from underground,
And flows as lava all around …
Listen now,
Don't interrupt,
When volcanoes blow,
They do erupt!

From: sciencepoems.net

Procedure

Pets

Lainey's Intro

Hey! How are you all doing this week?

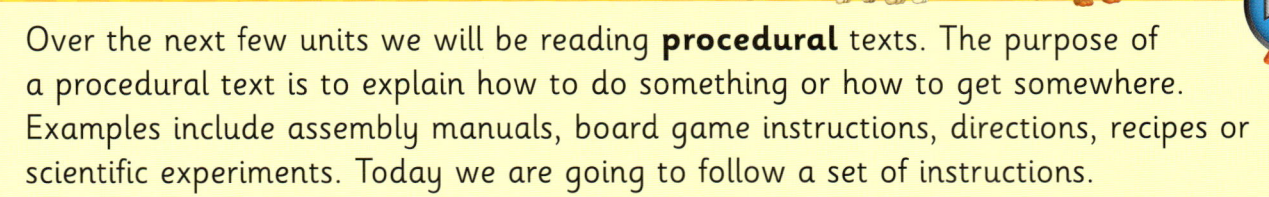

Over the next few units we will be reading **procedural** texts. The purpose of a procedural text is to explain how to do something or how to get somewhere. Examples include assembly manuals, board game instructions, directions, recipes or scientific experiments. Today we are going to follow a set of instructions.

Procedural texts include certain features. Let's examine the features that would be included in a set of instructions:

- **Title:** Name of the procedure.
- **Goal:** Purpose of the procedure.
- **Materials:** The materials or equipment you will need.
- **Headings:** This breaks up the procedure into different parts.
- **Steps:** These tell the reader how to do something.
- **Conclusion:** This is a short statement that recaps the procedure.

I chose this text by the RSPCA because I really want a dog! I would love to have a Labrador. They are really friendly. Did you know that they are known as the original fishermen's friend? I have to persuade my mum to let me have a dog. She doesn't think I am responsible enough yet. I'm going to show her just how responsible I am by showing her my project on 'How to Care for a Dog'. I'm hoping she is going to be blown away by all the research I have done.

Transfer of skills: Pets bring lots of joy and fun to our lives. Do you know the word 'pets' in other languages? Let's take a look.
peataí (Irish), *haustiere* (German), *mascotas* (Spanish), *animaux domestiques* (French)

> **My reading goal** ★ Notice how procedural texts use verbs to give readers a clear understanding of how to do something.

How to Care for a Dog

Owning and caring for a dog can be great fun and very rewarding, but it's a big **responsibility** and a long-term commitment in terms of care and cost – typically dogs live for 13 years, but may live for much longer. If you are responsible for a dog, even on a **temporary** basis, you are required by law to care for him or her properly.

There is no one 'perfect' way to care for all dogs because every dog and every situation is different. While many dogs are kept inside in their owner's home, some dogs are kept outside in kennels. It's up to you how you look after your dog, but you must take **reasonable** steps to ensure you meet all of his or her needs.

Under the Animal Welfare Act, pet owners are now legally **obliged** to care for their pets properly – as most owners already do – by providing the five basic welfare needs:

- A suitable place to live
- A healthy diet, including fresh clean water
- The ability to behave normally
- Appropriate company, including any need to be housed with, or apart from, other animals
- Protection from pain, suffering, injury and disease.

Hi Mum,

Please, please, please can I have a dog? I completed a project on how to care for my dog just for you! Will you read it and let me know what you think? I have researched it thoroughly and have thought of all the steps.

I can't wait to hear your thoughts.

Love,

Lainey

PS Did I tell you – you are the best mum ever!

The Environment

Title: How to Provide a Suitable Environment for Your Dog

Goal: These instructions will help you to provide a safe, suitable environment for the dog.

Materials: Bed, toys, crate

Steps

- First, provide a comfortable, dry, <u>draught-free</u>, clean and quiet place for the dog to snooze in. Look for a bed that is easy to clean and big enough to allow the dog to go through his or her natural **routine** of turning around before settling. Make sure that it is the right size and that it is made of material that is safe for the dog.
- Offer lots of suitable objects to play with and chew.
- Provide a dog crate. This can provide an open den area, which some dogs like to use as a safe place where they feel secure.
- Never use a crate as punishment or to prevent unwanted behaviour.
- Use the crate for three purposes: a den area, a place of recovery after surgery or to keep dogs secure and comfortable while travelling.
- Ensure the dog can exercise outdoors every day and can play and interact with humans or other dogs.

Conclusion

It is essential that there is a warm, clean place for the dog to sleep. Dogs are **inquisitive** and playful, so it is important that there are plenty of entertaining toys or activities. It is advised that dogs are given regular exercise.

Fact

Dogs are intelligent, so if they get bored and don't have enough to do, they can suffer. The RSPCA advises against keeping dogs outside because it can be very difficult to meet their needs. Living in a cold or wet place can cause a dog to suffer and may lead to illness.

> **Title:** How to Provide a Balanced Diet for Your Dog
>
> **Goal:** These instructions will help you to make sure that your dog has a well-balanced diet.
>
> **Materials:** Food (dry or wet dog food), dog bowl

Diet

Steps

- Ask the vet for advice on what and how much food to feed the dog.
- Feed the dog dry or wet food at least once a day.
- Read the manufacturer's instructions on the food and supervise mealtimes.
- Ensure that there is enough fresh, clean drinking water, especially if you are using dry food, as it can make the dog very thirsty.
- Provide a balanced diet and stick to it.

Conclusion

It is important to provide a well-balanced diet to ensure the dog stays fit and healthy.

> **Fact**
>
> Changing a dog's diet can lead to upset stomachs. Most human meals don't provide a dog with the nutrition it needs, and some foods, such as chocolate, onions, grapes and raisins, can be poisonous to dogs.

Protecting the Dog

> **Title:** How to Keep Your Dog Healthy
>
> **Goal:** These instructions will help you to make sure your dog is protected from pain, suffering and disease.
>
> **Materials:** Veterinary clinic, grooming brush

Steps

- Check the dog for signs of illnesses every day and make sure someone does this if you are away. If you suspect the dog is in pain, ill or injured, bring it to the vet **immediately**.
- Take the dog for a routine health check at least once a year.
- Ask the vet for advice about things you can do to protect the dog's health, including essential vaccinations and treatments to control **parasites**, i.e. lice or worms.
- Only use medicines that have been prescribed for the dog.
- Groom the dog's coat on a regular basis to keep it in good condition.

Conclusion

It is important to provide the best care for the dog.

Being Left Alone

Title: How to Prepare Your Dog to Be Left Alone

Goal: These instructions will help you to prepare the dog for being left alone.

Materials: Food, water, toys

Steps

- Teach the dog right from the start that being alone is enjoyable.
- Always feed the dog before you leave them alone.
- Ensure that the dog has to access to fresh, clean water while you are away.
- Exercise the dog before leaving them – go for a short walk.
- Give the dog something to entertain themselves with while you are away, for example a special toy or treat that they love, such as a ball or 'Kong' stuffed with food.
- Never leave the dog alone for so long that they become **distressed**.
- Leave your dog with family or friends if you are absent for a long period.
- Do not react badly if the dog misbehaves while you are out. The dog will link any punishment with your return rather than the destruction, barking or toileting carried out while you were away. The dog will then become anxious about the next time when you return after she or he is left alone, thus making the problem worse.

Conclusion

It is important that the dog is well looked after in your absence. It is essential that the dog is not physically punished or shouted at if there is a mess when you come home.

Fact

Many dogs who have been punished in the past when their owners return will show **submission** in an attempt to appease their owners. They make themselves as small as possible, putting their ears back and their tail between their legs.

On the Move

Title: How to Transport Your Dog

Goal: These instructions will help you to make sure that your dog is comfortable and safe while on the move.

Materials: Water, food, lead

Steps

- On a long car journey, make sure you stop regularly.
- Allow the dog access to fresh, cool water to drink.
- Provide food for the dog.
- Allow the dog to exercise and go to the toilet.
- Never leave a dog alone in a car.

Conclusion

It is important that you are organised and prepared before you go on long journey with a dog. Prepare a checklist, organise the materials you need and bring them in the car to ensure that the dog has a comfortable, safe journey.

Fact

It can get unbearably hot in a car on a sunny day, even when it's not that warm. In fact, when it's 22°C outside, the temperature inside a car can **soar** to 47°C within 60 minutes.

Dogs should always be able to move into a cool, **ventilated** environment if she or he is feeling hot and have access to water. Unlike humans, dogs pant to keep themselves cool. In a hot, stuffy car, dogs can't cool down – leaving a window open or a sunshield on your window screen won't keep your car cool enough. Dogs die in hot cars.

LAINEY'S RESPONSE

> I wonder if I have done enough to convince my mum to let me get a dog. What do you think? I think I have included all the procedural features. Can you skim back over the text and double check for me?

I have learned so much after completing this project. I'm really hoping that I have convinced my mum. I know how to provide a safe, clean environment for my dog and that I need to provide entertaining toys and exercise for the dog. I know how important it is to give the dog a well-balanced diet, how to check for pain or illnesses, how to prepare the dog for being left alone and how to prepare for a long car journey with the dog.

I'm thinking my dog will be my best friend for life. I can't wait to pet it, play with it, feed it and it bring it for walks. Does anybody have any pets? Can you give me any advice?

AUTHOR'S INTENT

What do you think the author wants you to understand after you have finished reading this unit?

Greedy Dog

by James Hurley

This dog will eat anything.
Apple cores and bacon fat,
Milk you poured out for the cat.
He likes the string that ties the roast
And relishes hot buttered toast.
Hide your chocolates! He's a thief,
He'll even eat your handkerchief.
And if you don't like sudden shocks,
Carefully conceal your socks.
Leave some soup without a lid
And you'll wish you never did.
When you think he must be full,
You find him gobbling bits of wool,
Orange peel or paper bags,
Dusters and old cleaning rags.

This dog will eat anything,
Except for mushrooms and cucumber.

Now what is wrong with those, I wonder.

Procedure

Magic Tricks

Evan's Intro

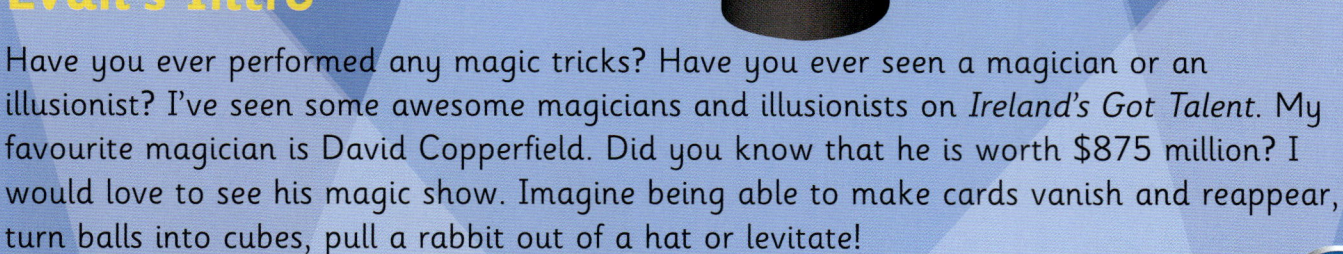

Have you ever performed any magic tricks? Have you ever seen a magician or an illusionist? I've seen some awesome magicians and illusionists on *Ireland's Got Talent*. My favourite magician is David Copperfield. Did you know that he is worth $875 million? I would love to see his magic show. Imagine being able to make cards vanish and reappear, turn balls into cubes, pull a rabbit out of a hat or levitate!

> It's time to have some fun! We are going to read some **procedural** texts. The purpose of a procedure is to tell the reader how to make or do something. The information will be presented in a series of steps.

In this extract from the book *101 Things to Do Before You Grow Up* by Laura Dower, you will learn how to do some magic tricks and how to communicate in secret by reading a set of instructions. Let's get reading and practising!

Transfer of skills: Can you say the word 'tricks' in other languages? Let's give it a go!

cleasa (Irish), *trucos* (Spanish), *des trucs* (French), *triukus* (Lithuanian), *tricks* (German)

> **My reading goal** ★ Pay attention to the sequence of instructions in order to do the tricks.

Trickery

Learn a No-Fail Card Trick

Title: The 'Who's Lying' Card Trick

What you need:

- A deck of cards
- A table

What you do:

1. Shuffle the deck of cards before your **audience** arrives. Make sure you know which card is on the bottom.

2. Once your audience is seated, fan out the deck of cards face down on the table and ask a volunteer to choose one card. They are not to show it to you or tell you what it is.

3. While the **volunteer** looks at the card, you should close the fan of cards, straighten the deck and place it on the table, face down. Ask the volunteer to cut the deck into two equal piles. Now ask your volunteer to put their card on the pile they cut from the top of the deck.

4. Place the other half of the deck on top of the volunteer's card. This should mean that the card you **memorised**, which was at the bottom of the pile a minute ago, is now on top of the selected card.

5. Now it's time for some good magician's patter. Explain to the audience that this deck of cards is special – it can **detect** lies.

6. Explain to your volunteer that you are going to turn each card over and ask them if this is the card they selected. They are to say 'no' every time, even when you turn over the selected card. The deck of cards will 'tell' you when the volunteer is lying. Obviously, you are looking for the card you memorised – the card after it will be the selected card.

7. When you turn over the selected card and your volunteer says 'no', yell 'Liar!' loudly and watch the audience's reaction.

Master a Coin Trick

Title: The Master of Illusion

What you need:

- A pocketful of coins

What you do:

1. Make a show of taking a handful of coins from your pocket – let the audience see that the coins are real. Choose one coin and pretend to pick it up – you'll need to practise this! Return the coins to your pocket.

2. Throw the imaginary coin back and forth from one hand to the other, making a small slapping sound as you pretend to catch the coin each time. (Practise beforehand with a real coin so that you can get the sound right, but if you loosen your fingers and slap the heel of your palm as you 'catch' your coin, it should sound okay.)

3. Do this several times, then stop and pretend to hold the imaginary coin in one hand. Ask your audience to guess how it landed – 'Heads or tails?' Of course, upon opening your hand there is no coin. That's okay because the audience **assumes** it's now in your other hand.

4. Slowly open your other hand to reveal that there is no coin there either – and bow while your audience applauds.

Use a Code to Send a Secret Message

Scramble codes involve changing the order of letters.

Title: Scramble Code

What you need:
- Paper
- Pen
- An accomplice who knows the code

What you do:

1. Write a message, then group the letters into fours. So

    MISSION COMPLETED

    becomes

    MISS IONC OMPL ETED

2. Then reverse each group:

    SSIM CNOI LPMO DETE

3. Put them together again:

    SSIMCNOILPMODETE

4. You can now pass your message to your **accomplice**, who knows the code (scrambled, groups of four) and who can crack it to reveal your message.

Did you know?
Codes are a safe way to send messages without being understood by outsiders. Historically, codes have been used by secret agents, spies and in wartime.

Use a Substitution Code to Communicate in Secret

Substitution codes work on the principle of swapping letters for other letters or symbols.

Title: Caesar Shift

What you need:
- Two thin strips of paper
- A pen
- An accomplice who knows the key letter

What you do:

1. Make some code strips. The lowercase letters represent the real alphabet and the uppercase letters show your CODE alphabet. Write the real alphabet out twice in a row and the code alphabet once. Side by side, the uppercase 'A' is aligned with the first 'b' of the lowercase strip, as shown in the strips at the right.

2. To write your code, all you need to do is line up the code strips as you want them (in this case, 'a' becomes 'Z', but you can slide the strip to have another key, such as 'a' becomes 'D').

3. Now you can write your message. So

    help me
    becomes
    GDKO LD

    To make it more difficult for people trying to crack the code, you might like to stick the words together, to make GDKOLD. That way, your message will seem like a stream of **unintelligible** letters rather than words that can be guessed at.

4. You and your accomplice both need code strips and you both need to know the key letter in order for this to work.

> **Did you know?**
> This **method** of coding is called the Caesar shift, as it was Julius Caesar's preferred way to write secret messages.

Send Top-Secret Correspondence

Spies and secret service agents <u>have favoured</u> the use of invisible inks to communicate with their accomplices without being discovered by the enemy. What better way to send <u>top-secret correspondence</u>, which will remain hidden to your enemies even if it is **intercepted**?

Title: Send Messages in Invisible Ink

What you need:

- Normal writing paper
- Candle wax
- A sheet of thin paper (such as tracing paper)
- A wooden skewer
- Powder

What you do:

1. Write an **innocent** and **irrelevant** message on the normal writing paper. This will put **suspicious** people off the scent.

2. Rub the candle wax all over the thin sheet of paper until the paper is covered with a layer of wax.

3. Put the thin paper (waxed side down) on top of your writing paper.

4. Using the wooden skewer, press into the thin paper and write your real message on the unwaxed side. Remove the thin paper from your writing paper.

5. The writing paper will look the same, but your secret message will be there written in 'invisible' wax.

6. When your accomplice receives your note, they will be able to view it by sprinkling powder (such as powdered cocoa or talcum powder) over the paper, revealing your secret.

Did you know?

Carl Frederick Muller was a German spy who operated in Britain during World War One. Muller sent seemingly innocent letters (in English) to his accomplices, but used formaldehyde and lemon juice to write invisible messages in German between the lines of English text. He was eventually discovered and sentenced to death.

Evan's Response

> Wow! Magic isn't as easy as it looks. It takes a lot of practice and finesse. Did you master the card or coin trick? Were you able to crack some codes?

Secret codes have been used for centuries to send secret messages back and forth. The first known code in history was developed by Julius Caesar. I wonder who the first person was to crack his code.

As time went on, codes became more and more sophisticated. Technology began to be used to make more complicated codes. When the telegram was used to send messages, they charged by the word. You could write up to 10 letters in a word for the same price. To cut costs, people made up codes. A group of letters meant a certain phrase. If you stop and think about it, we still use codes in this way today. Just think about the last text message you sent!

How about making some codes? Will your classmates be able to crack the codes?

Author's Intent

Was the author trying to persuade, inform or entertain the reader? How do you know?

Do you think the author gave clear instructions?

Tricks

by Michael Rosen

Nearly every morning
my brother would lie in bed,
lift his hands up in the air
full stretch
then close his hands around an invisible bar.
'Ah, my magic bar,' he'd say.
Then he'd heave on the bar,
pull himself up,
until he was sitting up in bed.

Then he'd get up.
I said,
'You haven't got a magic bar above your bed.'
'I have,' he said.
'You haven't,' I said.
'Don't believe me then,' he said.
'I won't – don't worry,' I said.
'It doesn't make any difference to me
if you do or you don't,' he said,
and went out of the room.

'Magic bar!' I said.
'Mad. He hasn't got a magic bar.'
I made sure he'd gone downstairs,
then I walked over to his bed
and waved my hand about in the air
above his pillow.
'I knew it,' I said to myself.
'Didn't fool me for a moment.'

Procedure

Board Games

Meg and Mel's Intro

TO: fifthclass@ireland.com

SUBJECT: Procedure

Hi guys, how are you? This is our last week to read a procedural text. We've saved the best till last!

You now know that the purpose of **procedural** texts is to explain how to do something or how to get somewhere. Let's examine the features that would be included in a set of board game instructions:

- **Title:** Name of the game.
- **Object:** Purpose of the board game.
- **Equipment:** The board game and its contents.
- **Preparation:** How to set up the board game.
- **How to play:** These are steps that explain how to play the board game.
- **Rules:** These are rules that the players must follow.

We chose instructions from one of our favourite board games: Jumanji! Have you ever heard of it? It's so much fun to play. Did you know that this board game is actually based on a picture book that is also called *Jumanji*? It was made into a film in 1995. Can you figure out how long ago that was? It also got made into a TV series, and another film called *Jumanji: Welcome to the Jungle* was released in 2017. What's your favourite board game? Was it made into a film? Let's read about the book's amazing author and illustrator, Chris Van Allsburg.

Transfer of skills: Board games are fun to play and there is such a wide variety to choose from. What is your favourite board game? Can you say the phrase 'board games' in another language? What do you notice?

cluichí boird (Irish), *stolní hry* (Czech), *jeugos de mesa* (Spanish), *gemau bwrdd* (Welsh)

> **My reading goal** ★ Notice the structure and word choice in board game instructions to help me understand the game.

Jumanji

Chris Van Allsburg

Jumanji was written and illustrated by Chris Van Allsburg. Chris was born in Michigan on 18 June 1949. He has one sister, Karen. They lived in an old farmhouse next to a large creamery building. Chris's father ran the dairy creamery alongside Chris's three uncles.

Chris's family moved house when he was three years old. He spent time exploring fields and ponds. He walked to school every day. When Chris was in 6th grade his family moved again to the east side of Grand Rapids in Michigan.

During junior and high school, Chris did not take any art classes, as he was more interested in the areas of maths and science. However, that was going to change. A number of students each year would go on to the University of Michigan. Due to the high-achieving standards of the students in his high school, an **admissions officer** was sent out to the school to interview the students and admit them on the spot if they met the necessary **requirements**. Chris liked drawing and the admissions officer told him about the College of Architecture and Design, which included an art school. Chris decided he would like to go there, but the admissions officer pointed out that he had not studied any art. Outsmarting the officer, he told him that his artistic skills were so advanced that he studied **privately** and was also doing oil paintings. The officer wasn't entirely convinced, but when he asked him about Norman Rockwell (a famous painter/illustrator of magazines), he was delighted with Chris's response. Chris was instantly admitted and became an **official** art student of the University of Michigan in 1967. He majored in sculpture, where he learned bronze casting, wood carving and other techniques.

During university he met Lisa Morrison and he married her. She became an elementary teacher. Lisa used picture books teaching her 3rd grade class and encouraged Chris to make illustrations for his own picture books. Chris set aside some time and successfully published *The Garden of Abdul Gasazi* in 1979. Since then he has written and illustrated 19 books. He is the winner of two Caldecott Medals for *The Polar Express* and *Jumanji*.

Plot of *Jumanji*

Peter and Judy are left in the house while their parents go out for the evening. After playing with some toys, they become **restless** and decide to go to the park. In the park they find a jungle adventure board game called Jumanji and take it home to play. It has a clear set of instructions that once the board game is started, it must be finished or it will continue on and on forever: 'Do not begin unless you intend to finish.' Peter and Judy quickly learn that the dangers in the game spring to life in every corner of the house.

Interview

Interviewer: What is your name?

Chris: My name is Chris Van Allsburg.

Interviewer: What do you do?

Chris: I write stories and draw pictures to go with them.

Interviewer: How do you do this?

Chris: I get up in the morning and go to my **studio**. I take out my pencils and papers and get to work.

Interviewer: How did you come up with the idea for *Jumanji*?

Chris: I came up with the idea by thinking about visual ideas. Everyone has seen a rhinoceros and everyone has been in a dining room, but how many people have seen a rhinoceros in a dining room? They don't belong in the same place. So I had the idea of a jungle adventure game where when you roll the dice, things happen on the board that make the animals magically appear in the house. And not just the animals: the floods, the volcano, the lost guide. So I thought this will work. I have a goal as a picture maker to do these strange things and an idea – the magical board game.

How to Play the Jumanji Board Game

The Jumanji board game can be played by two to four players. It is recommended for players aged eight and above.

This game is determined by the chance roll of the dice that sets the players out on a deadly journey. By **decoding** rhyming messages that may spell disaster, saving a fellow player in danger or the players losing if the jungle overtakes them before they can finish the game and escape, the various **suspenseful** possibilities and the game's adventurous theme make Jumanji extremely fun to play.

Are you ready to play?

Object of the game: You need to reach the centre of the game board and be the first player to shout 'Jumanji!'

Equipment:

- 4 player pawns: rhino, elephant, crocodile and monkey
- Game board
- Removable decoder plate
- Rhino figure
- 4 rescue dice
- 30 danger cards
- Timer
- An 8-sided die

Preparation:

- Each player picks a pawn, then places their pawn on the corner of the game board that correlates to their pawn colour.
- Place the removable decoder plate in the centre of the board.
- Put the rhino figure at its home base.
- Each player selects a rescue die.
- Shuffle all the danger cards, then place them face down on the board in the area marked 'Draw'.

How to play: The player who suggested playing Jumanji will take the first turn. The player who begins will take the timer and roll the 8-sided die. They will then move their pawn along the path towards the centre of the board by moving the same number of spaces as shown by the face of the die. The timer and the die are then passed on to the player on the left.

On your turn, roll the die and move your pawn the number of spaces shown on the die. Follow the directions on the space on which you land. There are four types of spaces: Blank Spaces, Jungle Spaces, Rhino Spaces and Wait for Five or Eight Spaces.

Types of Spaces

Blank Spaces

You're in trouble in the jungle. Draw a danger card and slide it into the decoder in the middle of the board. This will reveal which symbol all the players need to roll in order to free you. The players only have eight seconds to roll either the matching symbol or an hourglass (which is like a 'wild card' and matches every symbol). All players must match their secret symbol to free you. If they do not, then you will have to move back the number of spaces revealed by the decoder in the top right corner of the card. If you are freed, you will remain in the same spot, but the other players get to move forward the number of spaces revealed on your card. They do not have to follow the rules of whatever spaces they land on in this case.

Jungle Spaces

All players are now trapped in the jungle. Everyone has to roll to rescue each other. The player who landed on the jungle space must draw a danger card and use the decoder to reveal the rescue symbol. The group has eight seconds to roll the matching rescue symbol (or the hourglass). If each player manages to roll the matching rescue symbol, all players advance forward. If one or two players fail, the danger card is placed on the doomsday grid on the board. The process must be repeated until all players successfully roll.

Rhino Spaces

Landing on this space allows you to place the rhino directly in front of another player. The rhino blocks the player's path and prevents them from moving forward unless they roll an even number on their turn. If you are a blocked player and roll an even number, move the rhino back to its home base and move forward by the number of spaces shown on the dice. If you are unable to roll an even number, remain on that space and follow the instructions for the space. If your pawn has to move backwards, the rhino moves with you and remains one space ahead of you.

Wait for Five or Eight Spaces

You are being sucked into the jungle. The player to your left needs to roll a 5 or 8 to stop this. If they do, you can stay put and your turn is over. If the player fails, you have to move back one space. The player will hand the die to the next player. They have to try to roll a 5 or 8 – if they fail, you will have to move back one space again. This will be repeated until somebody rolls a 5 or 8. You do not roll.

Rules

- The player to reach the game board centre first and yell 'Jumanji!' wins the game.
- You can reach the game board centre either by rolling the exact number required on the number die on your own turn or on a fellow player's turn by moving the exact number required after moving ahead on a danger count.

Meg and Mel's Response

Chris Van Allsburg is one talented man! Not only does he write his own picture books, he illustrates them too. We learned that a pretty cool technique he uses is putting visual images together that don't belong together. He is very creative. We would love to know what his favourite picture book is that he wrote and illustrated. We also wonder how many awards he has won. What questions would you like to ask him?

Let's take a look at the procedural features of the board game. Were the specific features used? What were they? Skim back over the extract and check.

Who knew that the *Jumanji* film is actually based on the picture book? Is it just us or is anyone else enticed to buy the game *Jumanji*? We wonder which is best, the picture book or the film.

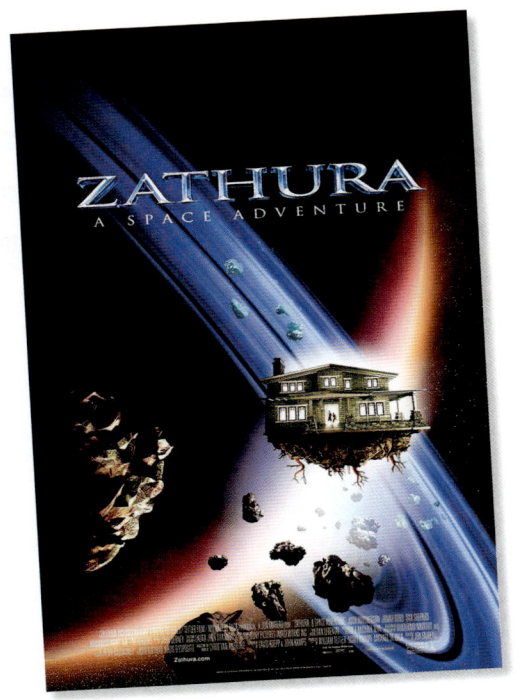

There is a sequel to the 1995 *Jumanji* film, called *Zathura*. We know what we'll be spending our weekend doing!

Author's Intent

Why do you think the author chose to write about a board game?

Do you think the author gave clear instructions? Were you able to follow the instructions?

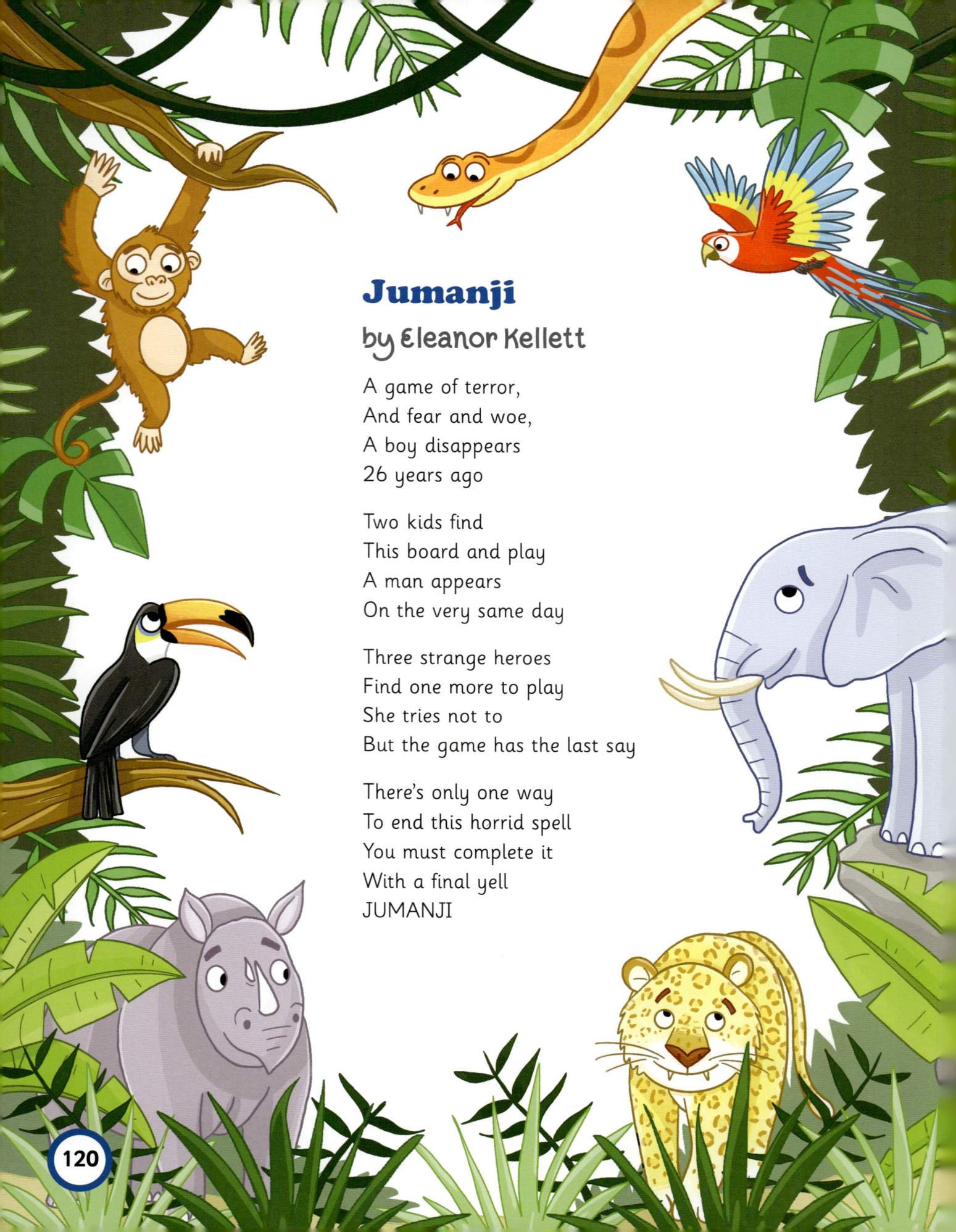

Jumanji

by Eleanor Kellett

A game of terror,
And fear and woe,
A boy disappears
26 years ago

Two kids find
This board and play
A man appears
On the very same day

Three strange heroes
Find one more to play
She tries not to
But the game has the last say

There's only one way
To end this horrid spell
You must complete it
With a final yell
JUMANJI

Report

Predators

Evan's Intro

Hey guys, *caidé mar atá sibh? Tá mé ar fheabhas!* Do you know what a predator is? Every creature needs to eat to survive, and for some that means eating other animals. To do this, they must be able to catch animals that really don't want to be eaten up as dinner. Do you have a favourite predator? My favourite predator is the ferocious lion.

Name: Lion
Classification: Mammal
Diet: Carnivore
Habitat: Desert, grassland
Life span: 10–14 years

Over the next few weeks we are going to be reading **reports**. Report writing is a type of informative writing. It gives information to the reader on a particular topic. Authors have to research their topic and write paragraphs that are organised by classification, description and a summarising comment. Be on the lookout for these features as we read reports on the world's strangest predators.

You are going to read five reports on predators from the book *World's Strangest Predators*. You will read about how they look and the cunning ways they try to catch their prey. What animal do you think is ranked as the number one world's strangest predator? Let's read on!

Transfer of skills: We don't know how many types of animals there are in the world. Why do you think this is? We *do* know that there are approximately 1.2 million known species of animals. Can you say the word 'animals' in other languages? What do you notice?

ainmhithe (Irish), *zwierząt* (Polish), *animals* (Spanish), *animaux* (French)

> **My reading goal** ★ Determine important information.

World's Strangest Predators

Box Jellyfish

Name: Box jellyfish
Classification: Invertebrate
Diet: Carnivore
Average life span: Less than one year
Size: 3 metres long, 25 cm across
Weight: Up to 2 kg

Box jellyfish are the most dangerous jellyfish in the world. Box jellies, also called sea wasps and **marine** stingers, live primarily in coastal waters off northern Australia and throughout the Indo-Pacific. Their average life span is less than a year.

All jellyfish are invertebrate animals. They do not have a backbone in their bodies. They are pale blue and **transparent** in colour and get their name from the cube-like shape of their bell. Up to 15 tentacles grow from each corner of the bell and can reach 3 metres in length. Each tentacle has about 5,000 stinging cells, which are triggered not by touch, but by the presence of a chemical on the outer layer of its prey.

The box jellyfish developed its frighteningly powerful **venom** to instantly stun or kill prey, like fish and shrimp, so their struggle to escape wouldn't damage its delicate tentacles. Their venom is considered to be among the most deadly in the world, containing **toxins** that attack the heart, nervous system and skin cells. It is so overpoweringly painful that human victims have been known to go into shock and drown or die of heart failure before even reaching shore. Survivors can experience considerable pain for weeks and often have significant scarring where the tentacles made contact.

> The box jellyfish is ranked #32 of the world's strangest predators.

Vampire Bat

Name: Vampire bat
Classification: Mammal
Diet: Carnivore
Average life span: 9–12 years
Size: Body: 9 cm; wingspan: 18 cm
Weight: 60 g

Bats are **mammals** that can fly. Vampire bats are the only mammals that feed entirely on blood. They live in dark caves, mines, tree hollows and abandoned buildings in Mexico and Central and South America. Their average life span is between nine and 12 years.

They are small, brown and have pointed ears and noses. Their front teeth are sharp and specially shaped to slice skin so blood can flow. Like all bat species, their wings are actually modified fingers. The membranes between the finger bones make up the wing.

Vampire bats are **nocturnal** creatures. During the darkest part of the night, common vampire bats emerge to hunt. They feed on blood from cows, pigs, horses and birds. They have heat sensors on their noses to help them find a good spot on an animal's body to feed. Rather than sucking blood, vampire bats make a small cut with their teeth and then lap up the flowing blood with their tongues. These bats are so light and **agile** that they are sometimes able to drink blood from an animal for more than 30 minutes without waking it up. The blood sucking does not hurt the animal, but their bites can cause nasty infections and disease.

> The vampire bat is ranked #27 of the world's strangest predators.

Komodo Dragon

Name: Komodo dragon
Classification: Reptile
Diet: Carnivore
Average life span: Up to 30 years
Size: Body: 3 metres
Weight: 70–140 kg

Komodo dragons are giant **reptiles**. They have been around for millions of years, but scientists didn't study them until about a hundred years ago. They are found only on Indonesia's Lesser Sunda Islands.

Komodo dragons are the biggest and heaviest lizards on Earth. Full-grown adults can reach 3 metres long and weigh more than 140 kilograms! Most weigh about 70 kilograms. They are powerful-looking reptiles with wide, flat heads, rounded snouts, bowed legs and huge, muscular tails. They have a clumsy, back-and-forth walk and their yellow tongues flick in and out constantly.

Komodo dragons will eat almost anything they find, including already dead animals, deer, water buffalo, pigs, smaller Komodo dragons and occasionally humans! When hunting, Komodo dragons rely on camouflage and patience, lying in bushes or tall grasses until a victim passes by. They pounce on their prey with powerful legs and sharp claws, then sink their jagged, shark-like teeth in. An animal that escapes the jaws of a Komodo won't feel lucky for long. Dragon saliva contains large amounts of **bacteria**, which poisons their victims, usually within 24 hours. Dragons will calmly follow their bitten prey for miles, using their keen sense of smell to find the corpse.

The Komodo dragon is ranked #20 of the world's strangest predators.

Great White Shark

Name: Great white shark
Classification: Fish
Diet: Carnivore
Average life span: Up to 70 years
Size: Body: 4.5–6 metres
Weight: 2.5 tonnes or more

Great whites are the largest predatory fish on Earth. They are found in cool, coastal waters throughout the world. Great white sharks have an endangered status.

They have slate-grey upper bodies to blend in with the rocky coastal sea floor, but they get their name from their universally white underbellies. They are streamlined, torpedo-shaped swimmers with powerful tails that can propel them through the water at speeds of up to 25 km per hour. They can even leave the water completely, breaching like whales when attacking prey from underneath.

Sharks count on the element of surprise as they hunt. When they see a seal at the surface of the water, sharks will often position themselves underneath the seal. Using their tails as propellers, they swim upward at a fast sprint, burst out of the water in a leap called a breach and fall back into the water with the seal in their mouths. They can smell a single drop of blood from up to 5 kilometres away. Sharks don't chew their food; they rip off chunks of meat and swallow them whole. They can last a month or two without another big meal.

The great white shark is rated #14 of the world's strangest predators.

Anaconda

Name: Anaconda
Classification: Reptile
Diet: Carnivore
Average life span: 10 years
Size: Body: 6–9 metres
Weight: Up to 227 kg

The green anaconda is a member of a family of snakes called constrictors. It is a **semi-aquatic** snake found in tropical South America.

It is the largest snake in the world, growing up to 9 m long and weighing as much as 227 kg. Picture it – that's longer than six 10-year-olds lying head to foot and heavier than all of them put together!

Anacondas live in swamps, marshes and slow-moving streams, mainly in the tropical rainforests of the Amazon and Orinoco basins. They are **cumbersome** on land, but stealthy and sleek in the water. Their eyes and nasal openings are on top of their heads, allowing them to lay in wait for prey while remaining nearly completely submerged.

They reach their monumental size on a diet of wild pigs, deer, birds, turtles, capybara, caimans and even jaguars. Anacondas are **non-venomous** constrictors, coiling their muscular bodies around captured prey and squeezing until the animal suffocates. Jaws attached by stretchy ligaments allow them to swallow their prey whole, no matter the size, and they can go weeks or months without food after a big meal.

The anaconda is rated #10 of the world's strangest predators.

Evan's Response

Cliff-hanger! We still don't know what the #1 world's strangest predator is. Frustrating or what? If you guessed the box jellyfish, vampire bat, Komodo dragon, great white shark or anaconda, you will have to guess again! Maybe it's an insect, a bird or even a plant. If you are dying to find out, I definitely recommend reading the book.

What did you think? Which predator did you most enjoy reading about?

I really enjoyed reading about the great white sharks. It's amazing that they can smell a single drop of blood from up to 5 kilometres away! What I find confusing is that they are at the top of the food chain and aren't likely to be killed by other sea creatures, yet they are on the endangered species list. I wonder why this is?

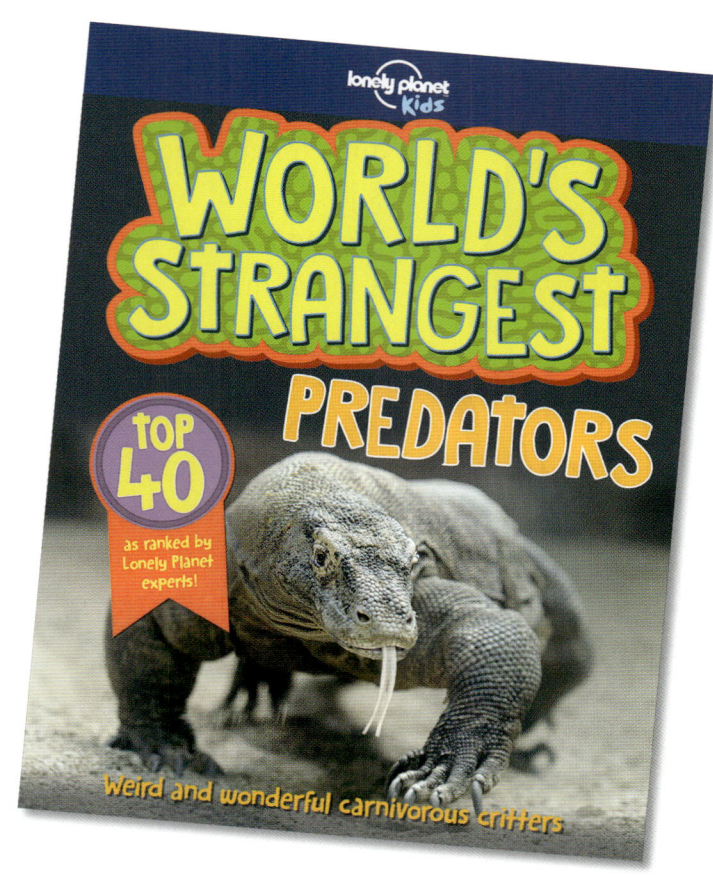

Now I have to write my animal report on lions!

Author's Intent
Did the author effectively give information? Why do you think this?

Predator

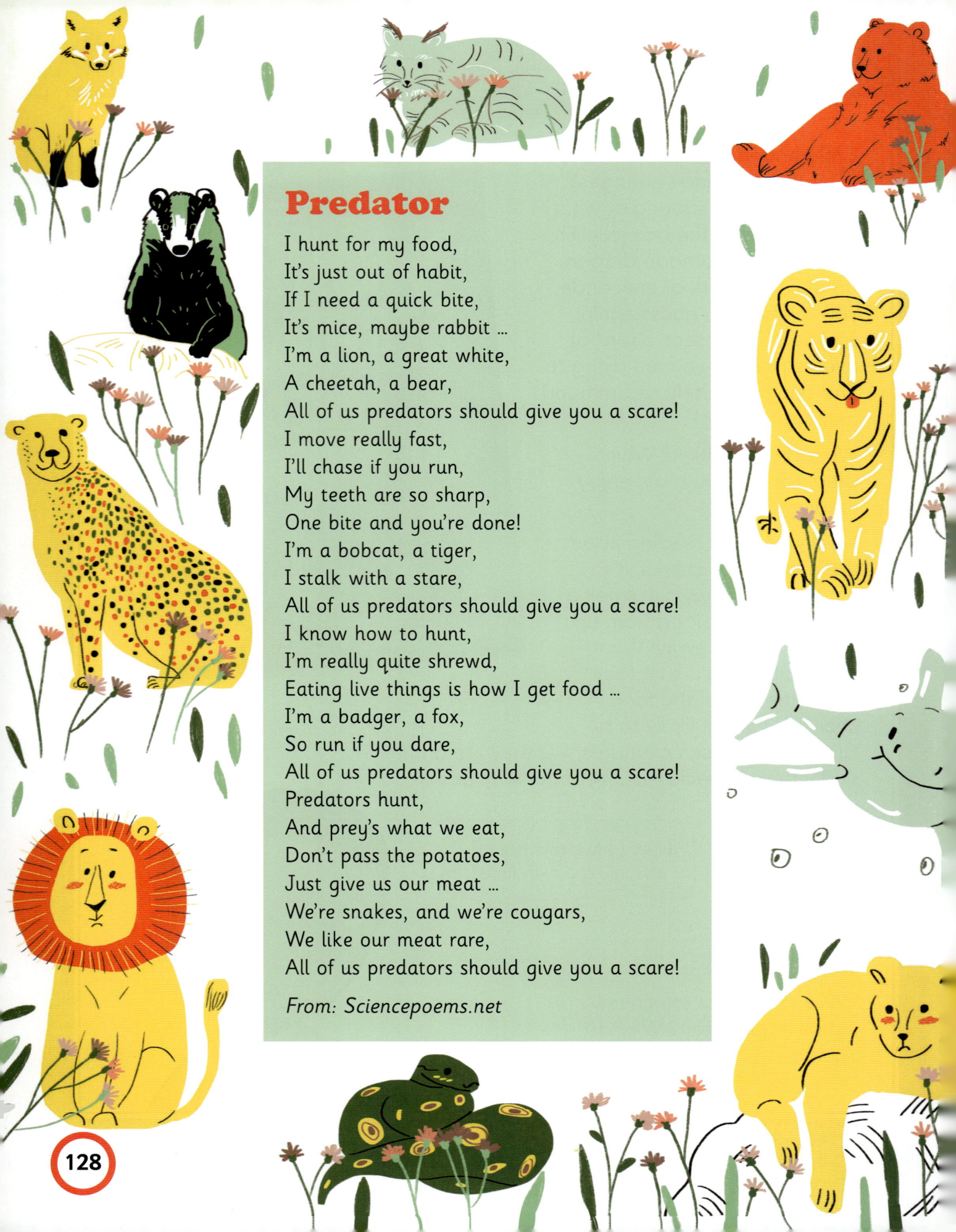

I hunt for my food,
It's just out of habit,
If I need a quick bite,
It's mice, maybe rabbit …
I'm a lion, a great white,
A cheetah, a bear,
All of us predators should give you a scare!
I move really fast,
I'll chase if you run,
My teeth are so sharp,
One bite and you're done!
I'm a bobcat, a tiger,
I stalk with a stare,
All of us predators should give you a scare!
I know how to hunt,
I'm really quite shrewd,
Eating live things is how I get food …
I'm a badger, a fox,
So run if you dare,
All of us predators should give you a scare!
Predators hunt,
And prey's what we eat,
Don't pass the potatoes,
Just give us our meat …
We're snakes, and we're cougars,
We like our meat rare,
All of us predators should give you a scare!

From: Sciencepoems.net

Report

Famous Buildings

Ella's Intro

Hi guys! Have you ever visited any famous buildings? Do you know who designed them?

People who design buildings are called architects. Architects express an artistic vision through the size, shape, colour, materials and style of a building's elements. But unlike painters or sculptors, who can create a work of art for its own sake, architects must design a building for a specific purpose. The architect can produce a work of art, but it must also be functional.

There are different types of architecture, including classical, Romanesque, Gothic and modernist architecture. Can you guess which types the buildings in this extract are?

We will read about five famous buildings through **reports**. A report is a factual text. It gives us some amazing facts about these buildings. Some are very old and have been preserved, while some are more modern.

This week we are going to read extracts from *13 Buildings Children Should Know* by Annette Roeder. I've chosen five of the most famous buildings from around the world for you to marvel at. What famous building would you like to visit? I've always wanted to visit the Taj Mahal in India. Doesn't it look majestic?

Transfer of skills: The world has so many incredible buildings. They include monuments, cathedrals and other feats of amazing architecture. Can you say the word 'buildings' in other languages? What do you notice?

foirgnimh (Irish), *budynki* (Polish), *edificios* (Spanish), *budovy* (Czech)

My reading goal ★ Re-read information to self-correct.

13 Buildings Children Should Know

The Great Pyramid of Giza

The only one of the <u>Seven Wonders of the Ancient World</u> to have survived to this day, it is the biggest single building to ever have been constructed – and it was the highest in the world for the longest time. The Great Pyramid of Giza has broken lots of records!

To this very day, we don't quite know how the Egyptians managed to **construct** this enormous, perfect geometric miracle in stone over 4,000 years ago. You can still visit it on the **outskirts** of Cairo, the Egyptian capital.

What were the pyramids built for? How did the architects and **labourers** manage to pile the incredibly heavy stones on top of each other without the help of modern machines or electric power? No wonder that some people's imaginations run wild when it comes to this wonder of the ancient world: some talk about a huge observatory, of places of worship and of aliens who could move objects using nothing but the strength of their willpower.

Started: c. 2554 BCE

Location: Giza, Egypt

Commissioned by: Pharaoh Khufu

Height: 146.6 m, but today it is only 138.7 m high because the tip is missing

Length of each side: 230.3 m

Material: Limestone

Special features: Together with its two sister pyramids, this is the only one of the Seven Wonders of the Ancient World left today

The Great Pyramid of Giza was the main structure on a big burial site that had walls, temples and smaller pyramids for the queens. The ancient Egyptians even dug pits for the big boats that would carry the dead **pharaoh's** soul into the afterlife.

The Leaning Tower of Pisa

The bell tower (which is the official name of the leaning tower) has stood on Pisa's Cathedral Square for more than 800 years. That is not even a particularly long time: some buildings are much older. And yet every additional year is a little miracle when it comes to this bell tower because it has continued to defy gravity!

When the people of Pisa laid the foundation stone of their **campanile**, they actually wanted to build the tallest bell tower in Italy that would be a visible sign of their wealth and success. And if there was trouble with the neighbours, the well-off at least could take refuge there. It was to be 100 metres high. When they were building the third level, the labourers had to take to their heels very quickly; the ground gave way on one side and their great tower seemed about to fall over!

If you want to build high in the sky, you must first make sure that you have a solid foundation that will bear the entire building's weight – but the architect in Pisa hadn't thought of that. And so the thin bottom plate and the first three floors sank about 4 metres into the ground.

The local people were so shocked that they took a 100-year break from building. Then they built the next four floors. The new architect – not the one who had started work on the tower, of course – attempted to balance out the tilt, but that didn't really work and the tower leaned further and further to one side.

Started: 9 August 1173

Location: Pisa, Italy

1st architect: Bonanno Pisano, 1173–1184, Floors 1–3

2nd architect: Giovanni di Simone, 1274–1284, Floors 4–7

3rd architect: Tommaso Pisano, 1360, belfry

Height: 54 m

Style: Romanesque

Special features: The tower learns at an angle of 4.43°

The Eiffel Tower

Whenever you think of Paris, you think of the Eiffel Tower. When it was built to mark the great World's Fair in 1889, nobody would ever have thought that it would become the city's most famous landmark. Its main **opponents** criticised it as an 'ugly lamp post'!

Of course, we must remember that people's taste was different in those days. At about the same time, King Ludwig II was building Neuschwanstein Castle in the style of a medieval castle. In fact, historical building styles were very fashionable at the time, so that many old forms were frequently copied in architecture.

And then Gustave Eiffel came along and built this metal structure in the middle of Paris – a tower of steel **components**, just the bare skeleton without anything to cover it! But Mr Eiffel got his own way. He paid for the tower himself – and created Paris's most famous landmark.

It was originally planned that the Eiffel Tower would be **dismantled** after 20 years, but it turned out to be an excellent radio antenna and so they left it standing.

Started: 28 January 1887

Construction time: Two years

Location: Paris, France

Built by: Gustave Eiffel

Architect: Stephen Sauvestre

Height: 300 m

Style: Art deco

Material: Steel

Special features: 2.5 million rivets hold the steel together

The Chrysler Building

The Chrysler Building won the competition to become the tallest building in the world — by playing a trump card. The story of the Chrysler Building is like a detective story with a comic twist. After the invention of the steel skeleton structure for tall buildings, it seemed as if the sky was the limit. The automobile manufacturer Chrysler decided to build the tallest skyscraper in New York — but unfortunately, the head of the Bank of Manhattan had the same idea too!

And so an exciting neck-and-neck race began. Shortly before the two buildings were completed it looked as if the Bank of Manhattan building (283 metres) was going to be 1 metre taller than the Chrysler Building (282 metres). However, the architect of the Chrysler Building had a trump card hidden away out of sight: inside the building he had secretly screwed together and stored the 56-metre stainless steel top of the building.

It only took a few hours to mount the crowning glory on top of the Chrysler Building, which was now even taller than the Eiffel Tower. Millionaires can be remarkably childish at times! However, the Chrysler's Building's luck did not last long: within a year, the Empire State Building had set a new record at 381 metres.

Started: 19 September 1928

Construction time: Two years

Location: New York, USA

Built by: Chrysler Ltd

Architect: William Van Alen

Height: 319 m

Material: Reinforced concrete

Special features: Decorations in the shape of car parts

The Sydney Opera House

Melon skins or sharks' fins? The shells that cover the Sydney Opera House look like anything but normal roofs!

Some of the greatest buildings have caused the biggest arguments, most of which were about money. This was also the case with the Sydney Opera House. Because of their complicated shell shape, the roofs cost 100 million Australian dollars. Originally, they had been estimated at just 7 million!

The Danish architect Jørn Utzon left Australia after just half of the construction time was up and was not even invited to the **inauguration**. He was so annoyed that he took the plans for the **interior** work with him.

The **reconciliation** finally took place 43 years later. Jørn Utzon and his son were **commissioned** to work out the basis of future developments and possible alterations. At last, the building's 'real father' was in charge of his shell-shaped opera house again!

Started: 2 March 1959

Construction time: 14 years

Location: Sydney, Australia

Architect: Jørn Utzon

Surface area: 183 m × 118 m

Height: 67 m

Materials: Reinforced concrete; roofs covered with ceramic tiles

Special features: Australia's best-known building and one of its symbols. Over 1 million white-glazed ceramic tiles from Sweden were flown halfway around the world to Australia.

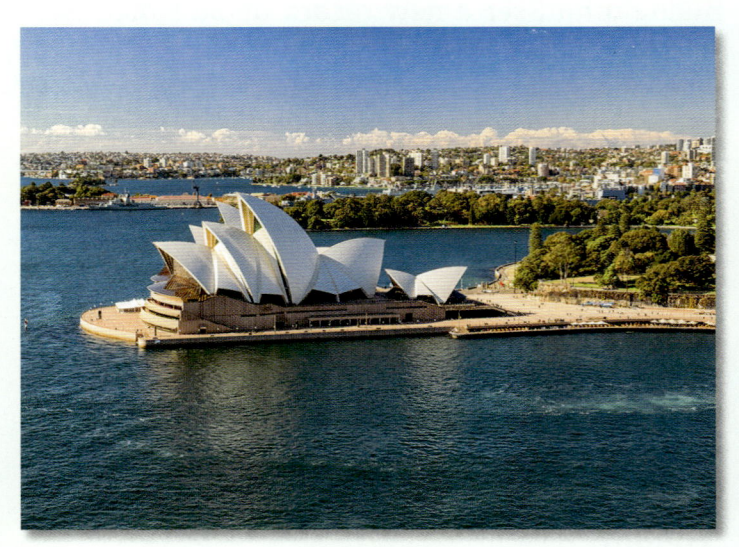

ELLA'S RESPONSE

Wow! What incredible feats of architecture.

Which building were you most inspired by? I am completely in awe of the Great Pyramid of Giza. It must have been backbreaking work to pile incredibly heavy stones on top of each other without modern technology. The Egyptians have such a fascinating history.

Did you know that people have tried again and again to straighten out the Leaning Tower of Pisa? Nobody has quite managed it though, which is why the Leaning Tower is as crooked as a banana as well as leaning to one side.

> I can't believe millionaires were acting like big kids. It must have been a very competitive race! I wonder how much the Chrysler Building cost to build?

I hope you enjoyed the extracts. Hopefully one day you will get to visit these amazing buildings – <u>the world is your oyster</u>!

AUTHOR'S INTENT
Why do you think the author chose to write about famous buildings?

Oh, How I'd Like to Travel

by Jodi Right

I lie awake each night
Staring at the ceiling
Following each crack
Finding new routes

Oh, how I'd like to travel
Somewhere new,
Somewhere old,
Somewhere where the people;
Sing merrily
Dance happily

Oh, how I'd like to travel
On a plane,
On a boat,
On something that will get me there;
Fast, like a soaring bird
Safely, like a locked room

Oh, how I'd like to travel
To see the sunset of a new horizon
To smell the sweet smells of newness
Like the delicious croissants;
Of France
Like the finest chocolates
Of Belgium
Like the mouth-watering tomatoes
Of Spain
To taste each one would full
A delicacy unknown to my taste buds.

Oh, how I'd like to travel
Could be anywhere
It doesn't have to be far
Because like every crack
It can be long route or,
It can be short route.

Report

Famous People

Tom's Intro

Dia daoibh, a chairde! Can you believe that we are on our last unit? The year has just flown! I hope you have enjoyed all the different text selections throughout the book.

> This week we are looking at biographical **reports**. A biography is an account of a person's life written by someone else. It is written in chronological order. It can include paragraphs on the person's early life, childhood, achievements, challenges and struggles or later life. It should always finish with a conclusion.

We are going to read some short sports biographies from *Young Heroes* by Lula Bridgeport. Who is your sporting hero? My Irish sporting hero is Cora Staunton and my international sporting hero is Usain Bolt.

Transfer of skills: There have been many international sporting heroes throughout sports history. Can you say 'sports heroes' in other languages? Let's take a look.
laochra spóirt (Irish), *sportowi bohaterowie* (Polish), *héroes del deporte* (Spanish), *héros sportifs* (French)

> **My reading goal** ★ Understand and determine what makes a sporting hero.

Young Heroes

Do you ever imagine what it would feel like to stand on the winners' **podium** at the Olympic Games or to lift a trophy at Wimbledon? Maybe you're <u>a natural</u> on the football pitch and you long to score the winning goal in the World Cup final. Or perhaps you dream of tackling the planet's biggest challenges, such as climbing Mount Everest or swimming the English Channel. If this sounds like you, then you could be on your way to <u>sporting glory</u>! But be prepared: it takes real commitment to become a champion. You'll need dedication, desire and drive to make it to the top. Endless hours of training are a must, while you also have to be mentally prepared for the testing times ahead.

But don't let the idea of all that hard work put you off – as the children in this section prove, taking part in sport of any kind can be rewarding. Not only will you get fit, make friends for life and have tons of fun along the way, you may also get the chance to represent your nation.

Take Pelé, Nadia Comaneci, Jahangir Khan and Michelle Kwan, **sensational** sportsmen and women who are not only superstars in their own countries, but all over the world. Or maybe you could follow in the record-breaking footsteps of Jordan Romero, Martina Hingis and Lydia Ko? With great talent comes great responsibility: sometimes, like Yusra Mardini, your chosen sport could make you a hero.

Each of these children will hopefully inspire you to get off your sofa, get outside and get active. You may even discover that you have what it takes to become a sports star of the future.

Yusra Mardini

1998 | Swimmer | Syria

Syria's Yusra Mardini is a talented swimmer with a **remarkable** past. By 14, she'd competed at the World Championships and was on course to a fantastic career. But all that changed when her country faced **civil war**. In 2015, Yusra's family home was destroyed and she and her sister, Sarah, fled Syria for Turkey. From there they travelled to Greece in a boat carrying 20 people. But not long into the **perilous** journey, the boat's motor failed and they were stranded. With little chance of rescue, Yusra and Sarah jumped into the sea and pushed the boat for three and a half hours, swimming the **refugees** to safety.

The pair eventually made it to Germany where, at 18, Yusra was selected to represent the first-ever Refugee Olympic Team, going on to win the opening heat of the 100 m butterfly at Rio in 2016. A true champion, Yusra is now a UN Refugee Agency Goodwill Ambassador.

Jahangir Khan

1963 | Squash | Pakistan

When Pakistan's Jahangir Khan was a child, doctors said he was too weak to ever play sport. But Jahangir grew up in a family of squash players and he was determined to prove the experts wrong. After training for many years with his father and brother, 15-year-old Jahangir gained enough strength and skill to enter the 1979 World Amateur Individual Championship, becoming the competition's youngest-ever winner. Then, at 17, he became the youngest-ever World Open Champion. But Jahangir wasn't done with breaking records – between 1981 and 1986 he won 555 matches in a row, the longest winning streak of any professional athlete in sport history!

Pelé

1940 | Football | Brazil

Today, a handful of world-class footballers compete for the title of 'Greatest Player on Earth'. But in the 1960s and 1970s, there was no debate. The greatest footballer in the world was Pelé.

Edson Arantes do Nascimento grew up in poverty. His family couldn't afford a real football, so the young Brazilian, who was nicknamed Pelé as a schoolboy, would practise his favourite sport with a grapefruit or a sock stuffed with newspaper. Pelé's natural talent shone through, making him the star of several local youth teams. His big break came in 1956 when, at just 15, he signed up to his first professional club, Santos. He immediately lived up to expectations, scoring in his **debut** game and becoming the league's top scorer of the season!

Within a year, Pelé was selected to represent Brazil in the 1958 World Cup. Brazil – and Pelé – had a sensational championship. At 17 years and 249 days old, not only did Pelé become the youngest footballer ever to play in a World Cup final match, but he also scored twice, helping Brazil to a 5-2 victory against host nation Sweden. His performance – including a hat trick against France in the semi-final – won him Young Player of the Tournament and made him a global icon.

For the rest of his career, Pelé created magic whenever he played. He is the most successful league-scorer in history, with 678 goals, while his speed, **stamina** and sheer power were **unrivalled** on the pitch. His flair and creative play won him millions of fans and three World Cup titles (the only player in history to achieve this). He was named Athlete of the Century and Footballer of the Century. To this day, he is still the greatest footballer the world has ever seen.

> 'Success is no accident. It is hard work, perseverance, learning, studying, sacrifice and most of all, love of what you are doing or learning to do.'

Martina Hingis

1980 | Tennis | Switzerland

Since turning professional at 14, Martina Hingis has won 25 Grand Slam titles! But the Swiss player is best known for her collection of 'youngest-ever' records. In 1993, 12-year-old Martina claimed victory in the girls' singles championships at the French Open, becoming the youngest player ever to win at a Grand Slam junior title.

Ricky Rubio

1990 | Basketball | Spain

Basketball's Ricky Rubio is a sensational sportsman. In 2005, at just 14, he became the youngest person to ever play in the Spanish basketball league. The following year, the junior Spanish national team won the International Basketball Federation's European Under-16 Championship. Ricky played so well that he was named Most Valuable Player of the tournament.

Lydia Ko

1997 | Golfer | New Zealand

Lydia Ko was always destined for greatness. She was five when she first picked up a golf club. By seven, she competed in her first golf competition – for adults! It was to be the first in a long line of major achievements. As an **amateur** player, Lydia claimed victory in the 2012 Bing Lee/Samsung New South Wales Women's Open, making her the youngest person ever to win a professional golf tour competition. In April 2014, she won her first LGPA tournament. Then in 2015, she broke another record – she became World No. 1, making her the youngest player, male or female, to achieve that goal.

Sports Prodigies

1896 Greek gymnast **Dimitrios Loundras** (1885–1970) is officially the youngest Olympian ever. He was just 10 when he won bronze at the first modern Olympic Games in Athens, Greece.

1936 The American diver **Marjorie Gestring** (1922–1992) holds the record for youngest-ever person to win gold at the Summer Olympics. She was just 13 years and 268 days old when she won the 3 m springboard diving event in Berlin in 1936. Marjorie's record will probably never be beaten because the minimum age for Olympic participants is now 16.

2000 Swimmer **Michael Phelps** (1985–) was just 15 when he represented the USA in the Sydney 2000 Olympics, making him the youngest US Olympic team member since 1932. The following year Michael set the first of hundreds of world records in the 200 m butterfly event at the World Aquatics Championships. He was the youngest male ever to set a swimming world record, at just 15 years and nine months. Michael also became the first athlete to win eight gold medals at a single Olympic Games (Beijing 2008), while he now has more Olympic medals than any other athlete in history.

2017 At 14, Japan's **Sota Fujii** (2002–), the youngest-ever professional shogi player (a Japanese version of chess), set the all-time record for games unbeaten when he won 29 shogi matches in a row.

TOM'S RESPONSE

Impressive or what?

Yusra Mardini's story stands out to me the most. Imagine having to push a boat for three and a half hours in dangerous waters. That took determination and courage. What a hero!

Imagine having to play soccer with a grapefruit or a sock filled with newspaper. Wasn't Pelé very resourceful? How lucky are we that we have footballs?

Who did you enjoy reading about?

So guys, remember that each and every one of you has talents. Find those talents and nurture them. Find what you love doing. Work hard and try your best. You never know – someday I may be writing about *you*!

I hope everyone has an awesome summer. I look forward to seeing you in Sixth Class!

Author's Intent

Why did the author write about sporting heroes?

What do you think the author wants readers to think about?

Wendy Wise
by Kenn Nesbitt

There was a girl named Wendy Wise,
who didn't like to exercise.
She wouldn't ever lift a weight,
or skip a rope, or roller skate.
You'd never see her ride a bike,
or bounce a ball, or take a hike.
She wouldn't run, or trot, or jog,
or go outside and walk the dog.
She wouldn't skip or climb a hill,
or practise any kind of skill
like jumping rope or playing ball.
She wouldn't exercise at all.

It's no surprise that Wendy Wise,
who didn't like to exercise,
would pass away one fateful day,
and in a rather tragic way.
You see, that day, up in the sky,
a tiny bird was flying by.
It lost a feather, small and brown,
that slowly, slowly drifted down,
and landed right on Wendy's head.
It knocked her down and killed her dead.
She was, it seems, so frail and weak,
with such a sickly, sad physique
that, when that feather touched her hair,
  it did her in, right then and there.

Poor Wendy! What an awful shame.
If only she had played a game,
or went outside to run around,
or practised jumping up and down,
or had a swim, or took a dive,
today she might still be alive.

Regrettably, it's now too late,
and Wendy Wise has met her fate.
But I, my friend, would much prefer
that you do not end up like her.
So please go out and play a game,
because, you see, despite her name,
to never, ever exercise
like Wendy, isn't very wise.

What Good Readers Do

Predict

Use clues to think about what will happen.

- I think/predict _____ because _____.

Question

What questions come up about the text, character, plot, detail or action?

- Who, what, when, where, how or why did the character …

Clarify

Clear up any confusion or reaffirm what is already known.

- I think the passage means …

Infer

Use clues from the text and what is known to figure out what the text means.

- Because _____ I think that …

Summarise

Explain what the text is mainly about.

- In my words, this is about …

Compare

Identify similarities seen in the text between characters or situations.

- I see how _____ is similar to _____ because …

Connect

Make connections in the text by explaining how one can relate to it or how the text relates to something else.

- I can relate to this because …
- This reminds me of …
- This is similar to _____ because …

Visualise

Pause to imagine what the setting or action must be like.

- When I was reading, I pictured …

Evaluate

Form an idea or judgement about the text.

- This is good/bad because …
- I would have done _____ differently because …
- I liked/didn't like the way the writer …

Synthesise

Put the pieces together to see them in a new way.

- All these details lead me to believe …
- Based on _____, the author wants me to think …

Poster Credit: Gerard Aflague Collection

Word Attack Strategies

Questions to ask when I don't understand what I read

When it doesn't sound right, ask yourself:

- ✓ Do I need to sound out the words?
- ✓ Do other words in the text give me clues to an unknown word?
- ✓ Does this sound like language?
- ✓ Do I need to slow down and re-read?
- ✓ What is the author trying to tell me?
- ✓ What is happening here?
- ✓ What do I already know that is like what the author is saying?
- ✓ What do I know about this kind of text?
- ✓ What is my purpose for reading?
- ✓ What is important for me to understand?

Good readers read every day.

Based on the work of Renaissance Learning

Reading Comprehension Strategies

Use background knowledge	Ask questions	Identify the author's purpose	Identify the main idea
Recognise sequence	Recognise cause and effect	Make inferences	Make predictions
Summarise	Distinguish between fact and opinion	Find facts and details	Recognise: compare and contrast
Make connections	Visualise	Re-read for clarity	Adjust your pacing

Based on the work of Hannah Braun, *The Classroom Key*

Literary Genres

GENRE	CHARACTERISTICS
Narrative • **Realistic** • **Fantasy**	Sequential story, characters, setting, plot entertains, may have dialogue, uses transition words, beginning, middle and end, expressive vocabulary
Informative • **Research report** • **Directions** • **Recipe**	Gives information, descriptions, factual, may contain steps, main topic and details, specific vocabulary
Persuasive or opinion	Trying to get someone to agree with your viewpoint, persuasive language, supportive facts, concluding statement
Functional • **Letter** • **Notes** • **Directions**	Useful, written for a specific purpose, factual, informative, precise vocabulary